CW00693139

Madeleines, Muffins & More

THE AUSTRALIAN
Women's Weekly

Contents

We have chosen some of very simplest recipes here – not too many ingredients and not too much to do to create the most perfect muffins, little cakes and those great French classics: madeleines. Get hold of a variety of baking tins for the best results – muffin pans, madeleine trays, or good non-stick baking trays and let your fingers do all the work – in just a few minutes! Enjoy!

Pamela Clark

Food director

Tips & techniques

Originally a breakfast food, muffins are these days a popular snack to be enjoyed with a cup of tea or coffee at any time of day. Available in both sweet and savoury versions, they can be served with or without butter. With a dusting of icing sugar and a scoop of ice-cream, sweet muffins can be dressed up as desserts. Add a side salad or a complementary flavoured butter and a savoury muffin becomes a delicious light lunch. Team them with soup and you have a satisfying lunch, supper or winter's dinner. It should be noted that the muffin recipes in this book are American-style muffins, a variety of quick bread, leavened with egg and self-raising flour. They shouldn't be confused with English muffins, which are the small, round yeast-risen breads.

MIXING

Muffins are quick and low-fuss to make and mostly require only a single bowl for the mixing. The butter is usually cubed and firm from the refrigerator when it is rubbed into the dry ingredients, then the flavourings lightly mixed in and finally the egg and milk or other liquid. Muffins toughen if the mixture is overhandled so the less mixing, the lighter the finished texture. Use a fork or a large metal spoon to cut the liquid through the dry ingredients and don't worry if the mix seems a bit lumpy — it will be fine when baked. If the recipe calls for berries, use frozen ones. If you add them straight from the freezer, there is less likelihood of them 'bleeding' into the mixture as they bake.

MUFFIN PANS

We used a medium (80ml) muffin pan and a large (180ml) muffin pan. Other sized muffin pans, including mini muffin pans of about 1 tablespoon

(20ml), are available and you will need to adjust cooking times if you choose a larger or smaller pan than the recipe specifies. Whatever sized pan you use, they should only be slightly more than half-filled with mixture to allow for rising. The pans should be lightly greased with a pastry brush dipped in melted butter or an even coating of cooking-oil spray. Or you can line the pans with paper cases — they come in every conceivable size these days.

TESTING IF COOKED

Muffins should be browned, risen and firm to the touch and beginning to shrink from the sides of the pan when they are cooked. If in doubt, insert a metal skewer into the muffin. It should be clean and free of mixture when it comes out. Turn the muffins onto a wire rack as soon as they are baked to prevent them becoming steamy. The exception to this advice is when the muffins are filled with custard, caramel or jam.

In this instance they should stand in the pans to cool for a few minutes before turning out. The fillings can be extremely hot.

KEEPING AND FREEZING

Muffins are at their best if eaten fresh from the oven while they are still warm. However, they can be kept in an airtight container for up to two days and frozen for up to three months. Place the cold muffins in a freezer bag or wrap individually in cling film or foil (depending on how you intend to reheat them), expelling as much air as possible by wrapping as tightly as possible or pressing the bag gently. To thaw in a conventional oven reheat foil-wrapped muffins by placing them in a single layer on an oven tray, in a moderate oven for about 20 minutes or until they are heated through. You can thaw muffins in a microwave oven, but as ovens vary in power, we can only give

general guidelines for timing. Reheat plastic-wrapped muffins, one at a time on DEFROST, MEDIUM LOW or 30% according to your oven. Allow about 45 seconds for one muffin.

Err on the conservative side with timing. You can always put them back in the microwave for a further short burst. Defrosted muffins should not feel hot to the touch. If they do, they are probably overheated and will toughen as they cool.

Flavoured butters

Many people consider butter the natural accompaniment to the muffin and we tend to agree. You can take butter one step further by creating complementary flavoured butters. Bring the butter to room temperature and beat in a small quantity of the flavouring. Wrap the flavoured butter in cling film, roll into a log shape and refrigerate until firm. Cut into rounds to serve with warmed muffins.

Sweet ideas:
- Crushed berries.
- Jam, honey or maple syrup.
- Honeycomb – crush first with a rolling pin.

Savoury alternatives:
- Roasted garlic – wrap unpeeled garlic cloves in foil and bake in a moderate oven until the garlic softens and can be squeezed from the clove. Mash it with a fork and mix into the softened butter.
- Finely chopped mixed herbs.
- Olives.
- Roasted peppers.
- Anchovies.

BUTTERMILK

Some of our recipes use buttermilk in place of milk. In spite of its name, buttermilk is low in fat, varying between 0.6 per cent and 2.0 per cent per 100ml. Originally the term given to the slightly sour liquid left after butter was churned from cream, today buttermilk is made from skimmed or semi-skimmed milk to which specific bacterial cultures have been added. It is readily available from supermarkets. Buttermilk not only adds a tangy flavour to cooking, its acid content also reacts with raising agents, giving some baked goods a lighter texture.

Sweet Muffins

Mixed berry dessert muffins

preparation time 10 minutes **cooking time** 35 minutes **makes** 6

2¼ cups (335g) self-raising flour

1 cup (220g) caster sugar

1 teaspoon vanilla extract

2 eggs, beaten lightly

100g butter, melted

1 cup (250ml) milk

1 teaspoon grated lemon rind

200g fresh or frozen mixed berries

1 Preheat oven to 200°C/180°C fan-assisted. Grease 6-hole large (180ml) muffin pan or spray six large disposable muffin cases and place on an oven tray.
2 Sift flour into large bowl; add sugar then combined extract, egg, butter, milk and rind. Add berries; stir through gently.
3 Divide muffin mixture among holes of prepared pans.
4 Bake muffins about 35 minutes. Stand muffins in pan for a few minutes before turning onto wire rack.

tip Muffins can be stored in an airtight container for up to 2 days or frozen for up to 2 months.

Blueberry & raspberry muffins

preparation time 10 minutes **cooking time** 20 minutes **makes** 12

2½ cups (375g) self-raising flour

90g cold butter, chopped

1 cup (220g) caster sugar

1¼ cups (310ml) buttermilk

1 egg, beaten lightly

100g fresh or frozen blueberries

100g fresh or frozen raspberries

1 Preheat oven to 180°C/160°C fan-assisted. Grease 12-hole (80ml) muffin pan or line with paper cases.

2 Sift flour into large bowl; rub in butter with fingertips. Stir in sugar, buttermilk and egg. Do not over-mix; mixture should be lumpy. Gently stir in berries. Spoon mixture into pan holes.

3 Bake muffins about 20 minutes. Stand in pan 5 minutes before turning onto wire rack.

VARIATIONS

lemon poppy seed Omit berries. Add 2 teaspoons lemon rind and 2 tablespoons poppy seeds with the sugar.

date & orange Omit berries. Substitute self-raising flour with 1 cup wholemeal self-raising flour and 1½ cups white self-raising flour. Add 1½ cups chopped dried dates and 2 teaspoons finely grated orange rind with the sugar.

choc chip & walnut Omit berries. Add ¾ cup dark chocolate chips and 1 cup coarsely chopped walnuts with the sugar.

Mixed-berry buttermilk muffins

preparation time 5 minutes **cooking time** 20 minutes **makes** 12

2½ cups (375g) self-raising flour

¾ cup (165g) caster sugar

1 egg, beaten lightly

1 teaspoon vanilla extract

⅔ cup (160ml) vegetable oil

¾ cup (180ml) buttermilk

200g frozen mixed berries

1 Preheat oven to 200°C/180°C fan-assisted. Grease 12-hole (80ml) muffin pan or line with paper cases.

2 Sift flour and sugar into large bowl; stir in remaining ingredients.

3 Spoon mixture into holes. Bake, uncovered, about 20 minutes. Turn onto wire rack to cool.

tips Use still-frozen berries to minimise 'bleeding' of colour into the mixture. We used 100g frozen raspberries, 50g frozen blueberries and 50g frozen blackberries in this recipe.

Blueberry muffins

preparation time 10 minutes cooking time 20 minutes makes 6

2 cups (300g) self-raising flour

¾ cup (150g) firmly packed brown sugar

1 cup (150g) fresh or frozen blueberries

1 egg, lightly beaten

¾ cup (180ml) buttermilk

½ cup (125ml) vegetable oil

1 Preheat oven to 200°C/180°C fan-assisted. Grease 6-hole large (180ml) muffin pan or line with paper cases.

2 Sift dry ingredients into large bowl, stir in remaining ingredients.

3 Divide mixture among pan holes; bake muffins about 20 minutes. Stand muffins in pan 5 minutes; turn onto wire rack to cool.

Blackberry streusel muffins

preparation time 10 minutes cooking time 20 minutes makes 12

2 cups (300g) self-raising flour

1¼ cups (170g) frozen blackberries

1 medium (150g) apple, peeled, coarsely grated

¾ cup (150g) firmly packed brown sugar

3 eggs, lightly beaten

⅓ cup (80ml) vegetable oil

⅓ cup (80ml) buttermilk

STREUSEL TOPPING

⅓ cup (50g) plain flour

2 tablespoons brown sugar

1 teaspoon mixed spice

30g butter

1 Preheat oven to 200°C/180°C fan-assisted. Grease 12-hole (80ml) muffin pan or line with paper cases.

2 Sift flour into large bowl, stir in remaining ingredients.

3 Divide mixture among pan holes. Coarsely grate streusel topping over muffins. Bake muffins about 20 minutes. Stand muffins in pan 5 minutes; turn onto wire rack to cool.

STREUSEL TOPPING Sift flour, sugar and spice into small bowl; rub in butter. Roll mixture into a ball, wrap in cling film, freeze until firm enough to grate.

Chocolate raspberry dessert muffins

preparation time 15 minutes **cooking time** 20 minutes **makes** 12

1¾ cups (260g) self-raising flour

¼ cup (25g) cocoa powder

¾ cup (165g) caster sugar

50g butter, melted

⅔ cup (160ml) milk

½ cup (120g) soured cream

2 eggs

½ cup (70g) coarsely chopped roasted hazelnuts

150g dark eating chocolate, chopped coarsely

1 cup (150g) frozen raspberries

1 Preheat oven to 200°C/180°C fan-assisted. Line 12-hole (80ml) muffin pan with paper cases.

2 Sift flour, cocoa and sugar into large bowl. Stir in the combined butter, milk, soured cream and eggs. Do not over-mix; mixture should be lumpy. Stir in remaining ingredients.

3 Divide mixture among paper cases. Bake about 20 minutes. Stand muffins 5 minutes before turning, top-side up, onto wire rack to cool.

tips These muffins are best served warm.

You can buy paper cases in an amazing range of colours and patterns. They are great for special occasions and will give your muffins a professional finish. We made our own freeform paper cases by pushing a 12cm square of paper (we used paper about the same thickness as printer paper) into ungreased pan holes, followed by a 12cm square of baking parchment.

Berry yogurt muffins

preparation time 10 minutes **cooking time** 20 minutes **makes** 6

1½ cups (225g) self-raising flour

⅓ cup (30g) rolled oats

3 eggs

¾ cup (165g) firmly packed brown sugar

¾ cup (200g) yogurt

⅓ cup (80ml) vegetable oil

180g fresh or frozen berries

1   Preheat oven to 200°C/180°C fan-assisted. Grease 6-hole large (180ml) muffin pan or line with paper cases.

2   Combine sifted flour with oats in medium bowl; stir in eggs, sugar, yogurt and oil. Do not over-mix; mixture should be lumpy. Gently stir in berries. Spoon mixture into pan holes.

3   Bake muffins about 20 minutes. Stand in pan 5 minutes before turning onto wire rack.

tips We used a mixture of raspberries and blueberries in these muffins.

Raspberry & coconut muffins

preparation time 10 minutes **cooking time** 20 minutes **makes** 12

2½ cups (375g) self-raising flour

90g butter, chopped

1 cup (220g) caster sugar

1¼ cups (310ml) buttermilk

1 egg, beaten lightly

⅓ cup (30g) desiccated coconut

150g fresh or frozen raspberries

2 tablespoons shredded coconut

1   Preheat oven to 200°C/180°C fan-assisted. Grease 12-hole (80ml) muffin pan or line with paper cases.

2   Sift flour into large bowl; rub in butter with fingertips. Add sugar, buttermilk, egg, desiccated coconut and raspberries; stir until just combined. Do not over-mix; mixture should be lumpy.

3   Spoon mixture into pan holes; sprinkle with shredded coconut.

4   Bake muffins about 20 minutes. Stand in pan 5 minutes before turning onto wire rack.

tip Two kinds of coconut – finely grated in the mix and shredded on top – create a moist morsel with a contrasting crunch.

Gluten-free, dairy-free raspberry muffins

preparation time 15 minutes **cooking time** 20 minutes **makes** 12

2½ cups (375g) gluten-free plain flour

1 tablespoon gluten-free baking powder

½ teaspoon bicarbonate of soda

⅓ cup (40g) rice bran

⅔ cup (150g) firmly packed brown sugar

1½ cups (375ml) soy milk

1 teaspoon vanilla extract

60g dairy-free spread, melted

2 eggs, beaten lightly

150g frozen raspberries

1 tablespoon coffee sugar crystals

1 Preheat oven to 200°C/180°C fan-assisted. Grease 12-hole (80ml) muffin pan or line with paper cases.

2 Sift flour, baking powder and soda into large bowl. Stir in bran, sugar, combined milk, extract, spread and egg until almost combined. Add raspberries, stir until just combined.

3 Spoon mixture into pan holes; sprinkle with coffee sugar crystals.

4 Bake muffins about 20 minutes. Stand in pan 5 minutes before turning onto wire rack.

Cherry coconut muffins

preparation time 10 minutes **cooking time** 20 minutes **makes** 12

2 cups (300g) self-raising flour

125g butter, chopped

1 cup (70g) shredded coconut

1 cup (210g) red glace cherries, halved

⅔ cup (150g) caster sugar

270ml can coconut milk

1 egg, lightly beaten

1 Preheat oven to 200°C/180°C fan-assisted. Grease 12-hole (80ml) muffin pan or line with paper cases.

2 Sift flour into large bowl, rub in butter. Stir in remaining ingredients.

3 Spoon mixture into prepared pan. Bake muffins about 20 minutes. Stand in pan 5 minutes before turning onto wire rack.

4 Sprinkle with a little extra toasted shredded coconut and sifted icing sugar, if desired.

sweet muffins

Banana & cinnamon muffins

preparation time 20 minutes **cooking time** 20 minutes **makes** 12

2 cups (300g) self-raising flour

⅓ cup (50g) plain flour

1 teaspoon ground cinnamon

½ teaspoon bicarbonate of soda

½ cup (110g) firmly packed brown sugar

1 cup (230g) mashed banana

2 eggs

¾ cup (180ml) buttermilk

⅓ cup (80ml) vegetable oil

½ teaspoon ground cinnamon, extra

CREAM CHEESE FROSTING

125g cream cheese, softened

¼ cup (40g) icing sugar

1 Preheat oven to 200°C/180°C fan-assisted. Grease 12-hole (80ml) muffin pan or line with paper cases.
2 Sift flours, cinnamon, bicarbonate of soda and sugar into large bowl; stir in banana then combined eggs, buttermilk and oil.
3 Divide mixture among pan holes; bake muffins about 20 minutes. Stand muffins in pan 5 minutes; turn onto wire rack to cool.
4 Make cream cheese frosting. Spread cold muffins with frosting; sprinkle with extra cinnamon.
CREAM CHEESE FROSTING Beat ingredients in small bowl with electric mixer until smooth.

tip You need 2 large over-ripe bananas (460g) for this recipe.

Never throw away bruised or blackened bananas: just pop them in the freezer as they are, to have on hand whenever you want to make this recipe again. Overripe frozen bananas can also be thawed and mashed for use in making banana bread, pancakes, breakfast smoothies or spread with peanut butter for a yummy sandwich.

Banana maple muffins

preparation time 15 minutes **cooking time** 25 minutes **makes** 12

2 cups (300g) self-raising flour

⅓ cup (50g) plain flour

½ teaspoon bicarbonate of soda

½ cup (110g) firmly packed brown sugar

¼ cup (60ml) maple-flavoured syrup

⅔ cup (150g) mashed banana

2 eggs, beaten lightly

1 cup (250ml) buttermilk

⅓ cup (80ml) vegetable oil

COCONUT TOPPING

15g butter

1 tablespoon maple-flavoured syrup

⅔ cup (30g) flaked coconut

1 Preheat oven to 200°C/180°C fan-assisted. Grease 12-hole (80ml) muffin pan or line with paper cases.

2 Make coconut topping.

3 Sift dry ingredients into large bowl. Stir in maple syrup and banana, then egg, buttermilk and oil. Do not over-mix; mixture should be lumpy. Spoon mixture into pan holes; sprinkle with coconut topping.

4 Bake muffins about 20 minutes. Stand in pan 5 minutes before turning onto wire rack.
COCONUT TOPPING Melt butter in small saucepan, add maple syrup and coconut; stir constantly over high heat until coconut is browned lightly. Remove from heat.

tip Serve with crispy bacon for a scrumptious brunch with a difference. You need approximately two medium (400g) over-ripe bananas for this recipe.

Banana muffins with crunchy topping

preparation time 20 minutes **cooking time** 20 minutes **makes** 12

1¾ cups (280g) wholemeal self-raising flour

¾ cup (165g) firmly packed brown sugar

1 cup (230g) mashed banana

1 egg, beaten lightly

1 cup (250ml) buttermilk

¼ cup (60ml) vegetable oil

CRUNCHY OAT TOPPING

1 cup (90g) rolled oats

½ teaspoon ground nutmeg

2 tablespoons honey

1 Preheat oven to 200°C/180°C fan-assisted. Grease 12-hole (80ml) muffin pan or line with paper cases.

2 Make crunchy oat topping.

3 Sift flour and sugar into large bowl; stir in banana, egg, buttermilk and oil. Divide mixture among prepared holes of muffin pan; sprinkle with topping. Bake muffins about 20 minutes. Stand in pan 5 minutes before turning onto wire rack to cool.
CRUNCHY OAT TOPPING Blend or process oats until coarsely chopped. Combine oats, nutmeg and honey in small bowl.

tip You need approximately two large (460g) over-ripe bananas for this recipe.

Banana, cranberry & macadamia muffins

preparation time 10 minutes **cooking time** 20 minutes **makes** 18

2¼ cups (335g) self-raising flour

¾ cup (165g) caster sugar

½ cup (65g) dried cranberries

½ cup (70g) coarsely chopped roasted unsalted macadamias

⅔ cup (150g) mashed banana

2 eggs, beaten lightly

1 cup (250ml) milk

½ cup (125ml) vegetable oil

1 Preheat oven to 200°C/180°C fan-assisted. Line three 6-hole (80ml) muffin pans with paper cases.

2 Sift flour and sugar into large bowl; stir in berries and nuts. Stir in the combined remaining ingredients; do not over-mix, mixture should be lumpy.

3 Divide mixture among pan holes. Bake muffins about 20 minutes. Stand in pan 5 minutes before turning, top-side up, onto wire rack to cool. Serve lightly dusted with sifted icing sugar.

tips Tou need two medium (400g) over-ripe bananas to get the required amount of mashed banana. We used freeform paper cases (see page 12).

VARIATION

banana, raisin & pecan muffins Omit the cranberries and replace with ½ cup coarsely chopped raisins. Omit the macadamias and replace with ½ cup coarsely chopped roasted pecans.

Native to Australia, buttery, rich macadamia nuts have a high fat content and should be kept, covered, in the refrigerator to prevent them becoming rancid. You can coarsely chop the same weight of other roasted nuts, such as pecans, almonds or walnuts, if you prefer, to use in place of the macadamias.

Apricot buttermilk muffins

preparation time 15 minutes (plus standing time) **cooking time** 20 minutes **makes** 12

1½ cups (225g) roughly chopped dried apricots

¼ cup (60ml) brandy

3 cups (450g) self-raising flour

125g butter, chopped

½ cup (110g) caster sugar

2 eggs, lightly beaten

¾ cup (180ml) buttermilk

APRICOT BUTTER

60g butter

1 cup (160g) icing sugar

1 tablespoon brandy

1 Preheat oven to 200°C/180°C fan-assisted. Grease 12-hole (80ml) muffin pan or line with paper cases. Combine apricots and brandy in bowl, stand 20 minutes. Process apricot mixture until finely chopped, reserve ¼ cup of apricot mixture.

2 Sift flour into large bowl, rub in butter. Stir in sugar, apricot mixture, eggs and buttermilk.

3 Spoon mixture into prepared pan. Bake muffins about 20 minutes. Stand in pan 5 minutes before turning, top-side up, onto wire rack to cool. Serve with apricot butter.

APRICOT BUTTER Beat butter in small bowl with electric mixer until as white as possible. Gradually beat in icing sugar, brandy and reserved apricot mixture.

Apricot muffins

preparation time 15 minutes (plus standing time) **cooking time** 20 minutes (plus cooling time) **makes** 12

1 cup (150g) coarsely chopped dried apricots

3 cups (450g) self-raising flour

½ cup (110g) caster sugar

125g butter, chopped coarsely

½ cup (125ml) milk

2 eggs

1 Preheat oven to 200°C/180°C fan-assisted. Grease 12-hole (80ml) muffin pan or line with paper cases.

2 Place apricots in small bowl; cover with boiling water. Cover; stand 30 minutes. Drain well.

3 Sift flour and sugar into large bowl; rub in butter using fingertips.

4 Add apricot to flour mixture.

5 Place milk and eggs in medium jug. Mix using fork; add to flour mixture. Mix again using fork until ingredients are just combined; do not over-mix. Mixture should be coarse and lumpy.

6 Spoon mixture into prepared pan. Bake muffins 20 minutes. tand in pan 5 minutes before turning, top-side up, onto wire rack to cool.

tip Muffins are at their best freshly cooked and eaten warm with butter.

Rhubarb & custard muffins

preparation time 20 minutes **cooking time** 30 minutes **makes** 12

2 cups (300g) self-raising flour

½ cup (75g) plain flour

¾ cup (165g) caster sugar

100g butter, melted

1 cup (250ml) milk

1 egg

3 cups (330g) finely chopped rhubarb

1 tablespoon demerara sugar

CUSTARD

2 tablespoons custard powder

¼ cup (55g) caster sugar

1 cup (250ml) milk

1 teaspoon vanilla extract

1 Make custard.

2 Preheat oven to 200°C/180°C fan-assisted. Line 12-hole (80ml) muffin pan with paper cases.

3 Sift flours and caster sugar into large bowl. Stir in the combined butter, milk and egg. Do not over-mix; mixture should be lumpy. Stir in half the rhubarb.

4 Divide half the mixture among paper cases; top with custard. Divide remaining mixture over custard. Sprinkle with remaining rhubarb and demerara sugar.

5 Bake muffins about 25 minutes. Stand in pan 5 minutes before turning, top-side up, onto wire rack to cool. Serve lightly dusted with sifted icing sugar.

CUSTARD Combine custard powder and sugar in small saucepan; gradually stir in milk. Stir mixture over medium heat until custard boils and thickens. Stir in extract; cool.

Thanks to hothouse growing, rhubarb is available all year, so you can indulge in these delicious muffins as well as any number of rhubarb desserts whenever you like. Be sure to discard every bit of the vegetable's leaf and use only the thinnest stalks (the thick ones tend to be stringy). You need five large stems of rhubarb to get the required amount of chopped rhubarb for this recipe.

Apple & custard muffins

preparation time 20 minutes **cooking time** 25 minutes **makes** 12

90g butter, melted

2 cups (300g) self-raising flour

1 cup (150g) plain flour

½ teaspoon ground cinnamon

¾ cup (165g) caster sugar

1 egg, beaten lightly

1 cup (250ml) milk

¼ cup (60ml) packaged thick custard

½ cup (110g) canned pie apples

2 tablespoons brown sugar

½ teaspoon ground cinnamon, extra

1 Preheat oven to 200°C/180°C fan-assisted. Grease 12-hole (80ml) muffin pan or line with paper cases.

2 Combine butter, flours, cinnamon, caster sugar, egg and milk in large bowl until just combined. Do not over-mix; mixture should be lumpy.

3 Spoon half the mixture into pan holes; make well in centre of each muffin, drop 1 level teaspoon of custard and 2 level teaspoons of apple into each well. Top with remaining muffin mixture; sprinkle with combined brown sugar and extra cinnamon.

4 Bake muffins about 25 minutes. Stand in pan 5 minutes before turning onto wire rack to cool.

Marmalade almond muffins

preparation time 15 minutes **cooking time** 20 minutes **makes** 12

2 cups (300g) self-raising flour

125g butter, chopped

1 cup (80g) flaked almonds

⅔ cup (150g) caster sugar

1 tablespoon finely grated orange rind

½ cup (170g) orange marmalade

2 eggs, beaten lightly

½ cup (125ml) milk

¼ cup (20g) flaked almonds, extra

ORANGE SYRUP

¼ cup (85g) orange marmalade

2 tablespoons water

1 Preheat oven to 200°C/180°C fan-assisted. Grease 12-hole (80ml) muffin pan.

2 Sift flour into large bowl, rub in butter. Stir in nuts, sugar and rind, then marmalade, egg and milk.

3 Divide mixture among holes of prepared pan; sprinkle with the extra nuts.

4 Bake muffins about 20 minutes. Stand muffins in pan 5 minutes before turning onto wire rack to cool.

5 Meanwhile, combine orange syrup ingredients in small bowl. Drizzle syrup over warm muffins.

Pear & ginger muffins

preparation time 15 minutes **cooking time** 20 minutes **makes** 12

2 cups (300g) self-raising flour

1 teaspoon ground ginger

¾ cup (165g) caster sugar

80g butter, melted

1 cup (280g) plain yogurt

2 eggs

2 medium pears (460g), peeled, chopped finely

MUESLI TOPPING

50g butter

2 tablespoons honey

2 cups (220g) unsweetened muesli

1 tablespoon finely chopped stem ginger

1 Preheat oven to 200°C/180°C fan-assisted. Line 12-hole (80ml) muffin pan with paper cases.
2 Make muesli topping.
3 Sift flour and ginger into large bowl; stir in sugar and the combined butter, yogurt and eggs. Do not over-mix; mixture should be lumpy. Gently stir in pears.
4 Spoon mixture into pan holes; spoon muesli topping onto muffin mixture. Bake about 20 minutes. Stand muffins 5 minutes before turning, top-side up, onto wire rack to cool.
MUESLI TOPPING Stir butter and honey in small saucepan over low heat until combined. Remove from heat; stir in muesli and stem ginger.

tips Buy a muesli that contains dried fruit to add colour and flavour to the muffins. We used freeform paper cases (see page 12).

Stem, or glacé ginger, is fresh ginger root preserved in a sugar syrup; it has a smooth, rich ginger flavour with an added hint of subtle heat. It can be eaten as a snack as well as (by far its most common use) used to add a flavourful burst of ginger when baking. Crystallised ginger can be substituted if rinsed with warm water and dried before using.

sweet muffins

31

Pineapple, passionfruit & mint muffins

preparation time 15 minutes **cooking time** 20 minutes **makes** 12

2 cups (300g) self-raising flour

125g butter, chopped

⅔ cup (150g) caster sugar

2 tablespoons chopped fresh mint

½ cup (115g) chopped glace pineapple

¼ cup (60ml) passionfruit pulp

½ cup (125ml) double cream

2 eggs, lightly beaten

YOGURT CREAM

½ cup (125ml) double cream

½ cup (125ml) plain yogurt

1 teaspoon grated orange rind

1 tablespoon passionfruit pulp

1 Preheat oven to 200°C/180°C fan-assisted. Grease 12-hole (80ml) muffin pan or line with paper cases.
2 Sift flour into large bowl, rub in butter. Stir in sugar, mint, pineapple, passionfruit pulp, cream and eggs.
3 Spoon mixture into prepared pan. Bake muffins about 20 minutes. Stand muffins in pan 5 minutes before turning onto wire rack to cool. Serve muffins filled with yogurt cream.
   YOGURT CREAM Combine cream and yogurt in small bowl, beat with electric mixer until soft peaks form. Fold in rind and passionfruit pulp.

tip You will need about 4 passionfruit for this recipe.

Pineapple ginger muffins

preparation time 15 minutes **cooking time** 20 minutes **makes** 12

2 cups (300g) self-raising flour

1 teaspoon ground ginger

125g butter, chopped

⅔ cup (150g) caster sugar

1 cup (90g) desiccated coconut

1/2 cup (115g) chopped stem ginger

1/2 cup (115g) chopped glacé pineapple

⅔ cup (160ml) milk

2 eggs, lightly beaten

¼ cup (60ml) golden syrup

GINGER CREAM

300ml whipping cream

3 teaspoons caster sugar

1 tablespoon finely chopped stem ginger

1 Preheat oven to 200°C/180°C fan-assisted. Grease 12-hole (80ml) muffin pan or line with paper cases.
2 Sift flour and ground ginger into large bowl, rub in butter. Stir in sugar, coconut, stem ginger and pineapple, then milk, eggs and golden syrup.
3 Spoon mixture into prepared pan. Bake muffins about 20 minutes. Stand muffins in pan 5 minutes before turning onto wire rack to cool. Serve with ginger cream.
   GINGER CREAM Beat cream and sugar together in small bowl until thick, stir in ginger.

sweet muffins

Apple streusel muffins

preparation time 20 minutes (plus freezing time) **cooking time** 20 minutes **makes** 12

40g butter

3 large apples (600g), peeled,
cut into 1cm pieces

⅓ cup (75g) firmly packed brown sugar

2 cups (300g) self-raising flour

1 teaspoon mixed spice

⅔ cup (150g) caster sugar

80g butter, melted, extra

¾ cup (180ml) buttermilk

1 egg

STREUSEL TOPPING

⅓ cup (50g) self-raising flour

⅓ cup (50g) plain flour

⅓ cup (75g) firmly packed brown sugar

½ teaspoon ground cinnamon

80g cold butter, chopped coarsely

1 Make streusel topping.
2 Meanwhile, melt butter in large frying pan; cook apple, stirring, about 5 minutes or until browned lightly. Add brown sugar; cook, stirring, about 5 minutes or until mixture thickens. Cool.
3 Preheat oven to 200°C/180°C fan-assisted. Line 12-hole (80ml) muffin pan with paper cases.
4 Sift flour, spice and sugar into large bowl. Stir in the combined extra butter, buttermilk and egg. Do not over-mix; mixture should be lumpy. Stir in half the apple mixture.
5 Divide mixture among pan holes; top with remaining apple mixture.
6 Coarsely grate streusel topping over muffin mixture. Bake about 20 minutes. Stand muffins 5 minutes before turning, top-side up, onto wire rack to cool.
   STREUSEL TOPPING Process flours, sugar and cinnamon until combined. Add butter; process until combined. Roll dough into ball, wrap in cling film; freeze about 15 minutes or until firm.

tip We used freeform paper cases (see page 12).

It is important not to overmix the muffin mixture; it requires minimum mixing and should look coarse and lumpy. Muffins are cooked when they are browned, risen, firm to touch and beginning to shrink from the sides of the tin. If in doubt, push a metal or wooden skewer into a muffin. When withdrawn, the skewer should be clean and free from muffin mixture.

sweet muffins

Lime syrup coconut muffins

preparation time 30 minutes cooking time 20 minutes makes 12

2½ cups (375g) self-raising flour

1 cup (90g) desiccated coconut

1 cup (220g) caster sugar

1 tablespoon finely grated lime rind

1 cup (250ml) buttermilk

125g butter, melted

2 eggs

LIME SYRUP

½ cup (110g) caster sugar

¼ cup (60ml) water

2 teaspoons finely grated lime rind

⅓ cup (80ml) lime juice

1 Preheat oven to 200°C/180°C fan-assisted. Grease 12-hole (80ml) muffin pan.

2 Combine flour, coconut and sugar in large bowl; stir in combined remaining ingredients. Do not over-mix; mixture should be lumpy. Spoon mixture into pan holes.

3 Bake muffins about 20 minutes.

4 Meanwhile, make lime syrup.

5 Transfer muffins to wire rack over tray; pour hot lime syrup over hot muffins. Drain syrup from tray and pour over muffins again.
   LIME SYRUP Stir ingredients in small saucepan over heat, without boiling, until sugar dissolves. Simmer, uncovered, without stirring, 2 minutes.

Citrus poppy seed muffins

preparation time 20 minutes cooking time 20 minutes makes 12

125g softened butter, chopped

2 teaspoons finely grated lemon rind

2 teaspoons finely grated lime rind

2 teaspoons finely grated orange rind

⅔ cup (150g) caster sugar

2 eggs, beaten lightly

2 cups (300g) self-raising flour

½ cup (125ml) milk

2 tablespoons poppy seeds

1 medium orange (240g)

icing sugar, for dusting

1 Preheat oven to 200°C/180°C fan-assisted. Grease 12-hole (80ml) muffin pan or line with paper cases.

2 Beat butter, rinds, caster sugar, egg, sifted flour and milk in medium bowl with electric mixer on low speed until just combined. Increase speed to medium; beat until mixture is just changed in colour. Stir in poppy seeds. Spoon mixture into pan holes.

3 Bake muffins about 20 minutes. Stand in pan 5 minutes before turning onto wire rack.

4 Meanwhile, peel rind thinly from orange, avoiding any white pith. Cut rind into thin strips. To serve, dust muffins with icing sugar; top with orange strips.

Wholemeal fig muffins

preparation time 10 minutes **cooking time** 20 minutes (plus cooling time) **makes** 12

2 cups (320g) wholemeal self-raising flour

1 cup (150g) self-raising flour

½ cup (110g) raw sugar

125g butter, chopped coarsely

1 cup (190g) coarsely chopped dried figs

2 eggs, beaten lightly

1 cup (250ml) milk

1 Preheat oven to 200°C/180°C fan-assisted. Grease 12-hole (80ml) muffin pan or line with paper cases.

2 Place flours in large bowl. Add sugar; rub in butter.

3 Add figs, then combined eggs and milk. Mix using fork until ingredients are just combined; do not over-mix. Mixture should be coarse and lumpy.

4 Spoon mixture into pan holes. Bake muffins 20 minutes. Stand in pan 5 minutes before turning onto wire rack to cool. Serve with butter and a drizzle of honey, if desired.

Orange & date dessert muffins

preparation time 10 minutes **cooking time** 20 minutes **makes** 12

2 cups (300g) self-raising flour

½ cup (75g) plain flour

½ teaspoon bicarbonate of soda

1¼ cups (250g) firmly packed brown sugar

125g butter, melted

1 cup (250ml) buttermilk

1 egg

2 teaspoons finely grated orange rind

1 cup (160g) coarsely chopped pitted dried dates

ORANGE SAUCE

¾ cup (150g) firmly packed brown sugar

2 teaspoons cornflour

⅓ cup (80ml) orange juice

2 tablespoons orange-flavoured liqueur

125g butter, chopped coarsely

1 tablespoon finely grated orange rind

1 Preheat oven to 200°C/180°C fan-assisted. Grease 12-hole (80ml) muffin pan or line with paper cases.

2 Sift flours, soda and sugar into large bowl. Stir in remaining ingredients. Do not over-mix. Spoon mixture into pan holes.

3 Bake muffins about 20 minutes. Stand in pan 5 minutes; turn, top-side up, onto wire rack.

4 Meanwhile, make orange sauce; serve with warm muffins.
ORANGE SAUCE Combine sugar and cornflour in small saucepan, gradually stir in juice and liqueur; bring to the boil, stirring until sauce boils and thickens. Stir in butter and rind.

Ginger date muffins with caramel sauce

preparation time 20 minutes **cooking time** 25 minutes **makes** 12

1 cup (160g) pitted chopped dates

⅓ cup (80ml) water

¼ teaspoon bicarbonate of soda

2 cups (300g) self-raising flour

1 cup (150g) plain flour

2 teaspoons ground ginger

½ teaspoon mixed spice

1 cup (220g) firmly packed brown sugar

2 teaspoons grated orange rind

1 egg, beaten lightly

1¼ cups (310ml) milk

¼ cup (60ml) vegetable oil

CARAMEL SAUCE

1 cup (220g) firmly packed brown sugar

1 cup (250ml) double cream

40g butter

1 Preheat oven to 200°C/180°C fan-assisted. Grease 12-hole (80ml) muffin pan or line with paper cases.
2 Combine dates and water in small saucepan, bring to a boil; remove from heat, add bicarbonate of soda, stand 5 minutes.
3 Meanwhile, sift dry ingredients into large bowl, stir in date mixture and remaining ingredients.
4 Divide mixture among holes of prepared pan.
5 Bake muffins about 20 minutes. Stand muffins in pan 5 minutes before turning onto wire rack to cool. Serve warm muffins drizzled with caramel sauce.
CARAMEL SAUCE Combine ingredients in medium saucepan. Stir over heat, without boiling, until sugar is dissolved, then simmer, without stirring, about 3 minutes or until thickened slightly.

The fruit of the date palm tree, dates are oval and plump, thin-skinned, with a honey-sweet flavour and sticky texture. They can be eaten fresh or dried, on their own or in prepared dishes. Just as you do when making a traditional sticky date pudding, soften the dates by standing them for several minutes in bicarbonate of soda dissolved in boiling water.

Overnight date & muesli muffins

preparation time 15 minutes cooking time 20 minutes (plus refrigeration time) makes 12

1¼ cups (185g) plain flour

1¼ cups (160g) toasted muesli

1 teaspoon ground cinnamon

1 teaspoon bicarbonate of soda

½ cup (110g) firmly packed brown sugar

½ cup (30g) unprocessed bran

¾ cup (120g) coarsely chopped pitted dates

1½ cups (375ml) buttermilk

½ cup (125ml) vegetable oil

1 egg, beaten lightly

1 Combine ingredients in large bowl, stir until just combined. Cover; refrigerate overnight.

2 Preheat oven to 200°C/180°C fan-assisted. Grease 12-hole (80ml) muffin pan or line with paper cases.

3 Divide mixture among muffin pan holes.

4 Bake muffins about 20 minutes. Stand in pan 5 minutes; turn, top-side up, onto wire rack to cool.

Overnight apricot & fig muffins

preparation time 15 minutes (plus refrigeration time) cooking time 30 minutes makes 4

⅔ cup (100g) coarsely chopped dried apricots

½ cup (95g) coarsely chopped dried figs

1⅓ cups (95g) All-Bran breakfast cereal

1½ cups (375ml) skimmed milk

1¼ cups (250g) firmly packed brown sugar

1½ tablespoons golden syrup

1¼ cups (185g) self-raising flour

½ cup (60g) pecans, chopped coarsely

1 Combine apricots, figs, cereal, milk, sugar and syrup in large bowl; mix well. Cover; refrigerate overnight.

2 Preheat oven to 200°C/180°C fan-assisted. Grease four holes only of a 6-hole large (180ml) muffin pan or line with paper cases.

3 Stir flour and nuts into apricot mixture. Spoon mixture into prepared pan. Bake muffins 30 minutes.

4 Serve muffins hot or cold, dusted with sifted icing sugar and topped with dried apricots, if desired.

sweet muffins

Date muffins with orange syrup

preparation time 15 minutes **cooking time** 20 minutes **makes** 12

1 cup (160g) wholemeal self-raising flour

1¼ cups (185g) white self-raising flour

1 cup (220g) caster sugar

100g butter, melted

1 cup (280g) plain yogurt

2 eggs

1 teaspoon finely grated orange rind

1½ cups (210g) coarsely chopped
pitted dried dates

ORANGE SYRUP

½ cup (110g) caster sugar

¼ cup (60ml) water

2 teaspoons finely grated orange rind

¼ cup (60ml) orange juice

1   Preheat oven to 200°C/180°C fan-assisted. Grease 12-hole (80ml) muffin pan with butter.

2   Sift flours and sugar into large bowl. Stir in combined butter, yogurt, eggs and rind. Do not over-mix; mixture should be lumpy. Stir in dates. Divide mixture among pan holes. Bake about 20 minutes.

3   Meanwhile, make orange syrup.

4   Stand muffins 2 minutes before turning, top-side up, onto wire rack. Stand rack over tray. Pierce muffins all over with skewer; pour hot orange syrup over hot muffins.

ORANGE SYRUP Stir ingredients in small saucepan over heat until sugar dissolves. Bring to the boil; reduce heat. Simmer, uncovered, 2 minutes.

VARIATION

fig muffins with orange syrup Omit the dates and replace them with 1 cup coarsely chopped dried figs.

Syrup muffins almost always have hot syrup poured over them when they're hot. Sometimes the syrup is poured over them while they're still in their pans, sometimes the muffins are turned out. In this case, the wire rack has a tray placed under it to catch the drips of syrup. This overflow syrup should be poured back over the muffins.

Chocolate brownie muffins

preparation time 15 minutes **cooking time** 20 minutes **makes** 12

2 cups (300g) self-raising flour

⅓ cup (35g) cocoa powder

⅓ cup (75g) caster sugar

60g butter, melted

½ cup (95g) chocolate chips

½ cup (75g) pistachios, chopped coarsely

½ cup (165g) chocolate hazelnut spread

1 egg, beaten lightly

¾ cup (180ml) milk

½ cup (120g) soured cream

1   Preheat oven to 200°C/180°C fan-assisted. Grease 12-hole (80ml) muffin pan or line with paper cases.
2   Sift dry ingredients into large bowl; stir in remaining ingredients. Do not over-mix; mixture should be lumpy. Spoon mixture into pan holes.
3   Bake muffins about 20 minutes. Stand in pan 5 minutes before turning onto wire rack. Dust with sifted extra cocoa, if you like.

tip Take care not to overcook these little indulgences – they should be slightly moist in the middle.

White chocolate & macadamia muffins

preparation time 10 minutes **cooking time** 25 minutes **makes** 6

2 cups (300g) self-raising flour

⅔ cup (150g) caster sugar

¾ cup (140g) white chocolate chips

½ cup (75g) coarsely chopped roasted macadamias

60g butter, melted

¾ cup (180ml) milk

1 egg

1   Preheat oven to 200°C/180°C fan-assisted. Grease 6-hole large (180ml) muffin pan or line with paper cases.
2   Sift flour and sugar into large bowl; stir in remaining ingredients. Do not over-mix. Spoon mixture into pan holes.
3   Bake muffins about 25 minutes. Stand muffins in pan 5 minutes; turn, top-side up, onto wire rack to cool.

Triple choc muffins

preparation time 15 minutes cooking time 20 minutes makes 12

1¾ cups (260g) self-raising flour

½ cup (50g) cocoa powder

¾ cup (165g) firmly packed brown sugar

½ cup (95g) dark chocolate chips

½ cup (95g) white chocolate chips

2 eggs

1 cup (250ml) buttermilk

⅔ cup (160ml) vegetable oil

12 white chocolate buttons

1 Preheat oven to 200ºC/180ºC fan-assisted. Line 12-hole (80ml) muffin pan with paper cases.

2 Sift flour and cocoa into large bowl; stir in sugar and chocolate chips. Stir in combined eggs, buttermilk and oil. Do not over-mix; mixture should be lumpy.

3 Divide mixture into paper cases. Bake muffins 20 minutes; remove from oven. Top each muffin with a chocolate button; bake a further 2 minutes.

4 Stand muffins in pan 5 minutes before turning, top-side up, onto wire rack to cool.

Choc-chip jaffa muffins

preparation time 10 minutes cooking time 20 minutes makes 12

2½ cups (375g) self-raising flour

100g cold butter, chopped finely

1 cup (220g) caster sugar

1¼ cups (310ml) buttermilk

1 egg

¾ cup (135g) dark chocolate chips

2 teaspoons finely grated orange rind

1 Preheat oven to 200ºC/180ºC fan-assisted. Grease 12-hole (80ml) muffin pan or line with paper cases.

2 Sift flour into large bowl; rub in butter. Stir in sugar, buttermilk and egg. Do not over-mix; mixture should be lumpy. Stir in chocolate chips and rind.

3 Divide mixture into pan holes; bake about 20 minutes. Stand muffins in pan 5 minutes before turning, top-side up, onto wire rack to cool.

Pecan & chocolate brownie muffins

preparation time 15 minutes **cooking time** 25 minutes **makes** 8

80g butter, chopped

150g dark eating chocolate, chopped

¾ cup (165g) firmly packed brown sugar

2 eggs, beaten lightly

1 teaspoon vanilla extract

⅔ cup (100g) plain flour

1 tablespoon cocoa powder

50g dark eating chocolate, chopped, extra

¼ cup (30g) chopped pecans

1 Preheat oven to 200ºC/180ºC fan-assisted. Grease eight holes of a 12-hole (80ml) muffin pan; line bases with rounds of baking parchment.

2 Combine butter, chocolate and sugar in medium heavy-based saucepan; stir over low heat until smooth.

3 Transfer mixture to large bowl; stir in egg, extract, sifted flour and cocoa, then extra chocolate. Divide mixture among holes of prepared pan. Sprinkle with nuts; bake muffins about 20 minutes. Stand in pan for 5 minutes before turning onto wire rack to cool.

Like walnuts but sweeter and milder, pecans are golden-brown, buttery and rich. Native to the United States, they are best known in the pecan pie of the American south but are good in both savoury and sweet dishes. Try them in salads, with soft cheeses, celery or apple, in cakes, cookies and breads.

Choc honeycomb muffins

preparation time 15 minutes **cooking time** 20 minutes **makes** 8

2 cups (300g) self-raising flour

¼ cup (55g) caster sugar

1 cup (190g) white chocolate chips

100g chocolate-coated honeycomb bar, chopped

1 egg, lightly beaten

60g butter, melted

1 cup (250ml) buttermilk

¼ cup (60ml) honey

1 teaspoon vanilla essence

1 Preheat oven to 200°C/180°C fan-assisted. Grease 12-hole (80ml) muffin pan or line with paper cases.

2 Sift flour and sugar into large bowl, stir in chocolate chips and honeycomb, then remaining ingredients.

3 Spoon mixture into prepared pan. Bake muffins about 20 minutes before turning, top-side up, onto wire rack to cool.

Chocolate hazelnut muffins

preparation time 15 minutes **cooking time** 20 minutes **makes** 12

2½ cups (375g) self-raising flour

½ teaspoon bicarbonate of soda

¼ cup (25g) cocoa powder

½ cup (100g) firmly packed brown sugar

125g butter, melted

2 eggs, lightly beaten

1 cup (250ml) buttermilk

1 cup (250ml) chocolate hazelnut spread

1 Preheat oven to 200°C/180°C fan-assisted. Grease 12-hole (80ml) muffin pan or line with paper cases.

2 Sift dry ingredients into large bowl, stir in butter, eggs and buttermilk.

3 Spoon one-third of the mixture into prepared pan, top with 1 level tablespoon of chocolate hazelnut spread. Top with remaining mixture.

4 Bake muffins about 20 minutes before turning, top-side up, onto wire rack to cool.

Butterscotch pecan muffins

preparation time 15 minutes **cooking time** 25 minutes **makes** 12

¾ cup (240g) dulce de leche

2 cups (300g) self-raising flour

¾ cup (165g) firmly packed brown sugar

¾ cup (90g) coarsely chopped roasted pecans

80g butter, melted

1 cup (250ml) buttermilk

1 egg

1 Preheat oven to 200°C/180°C fan-assisted. Line 12-hole (80ml) muffin pan with paper cases.

2 Stir dulce de leche in small saucepan over low heat until smooth. Cool 5 minutes.

3 Meanwhile sift flour and sugar into large bowl. Stir in nuts and the combined butter, buttermilk and egg. Do not over-mix; mixture should be lumpy.

4 Divide half the mixture among paper cases. Spoon half the caramel over muffin mixture; top with remaining mixture then caramel. Using a skewer, gently swirl caramel into muffin mixture. Bake about 20 minutes. Stand muffins 5 minutes before turning, top-side up, onto wire rack to cool.

Honey sultana & pecan muffins

preparation time 15 minutes **cooking time** 25 minutes **makes** 12

2 cups (300g) self-raising flour

2 teaspoons ground cinnamon

¾ cup (150g) firmly packed brown sugar

½ cup (50g) chopped pecans

½ cup (80g) sultanas

¼ cup (90g) honey

¾ cup (170g) mashed banana

¼ cup (70g) low-fat yogurt

¾ cup (180ml) semi-skimmed milk

2 eggs, beaten lightly

1 Preheat oven to 200°C/180°C fan-assisted. Grease 12-hole (80ml) muffin pan or line with paper cases.

2 Sift flour and cinnamon into large bowl. Add sugar, nuts and sultanas, then combined remaining ingredients; stir until just combined. Do not over-mix; mixture should be lumpy. Spoon mixture into pan holes.

3 Bake muffins about 25 minutes. Stand in pan 5 minutes before turning onto wire rack. Dust with sifted icing sugar and top with a light sprinkling of cinnamon, if you like.

tip You will need about 2 medium over-ripe bananas (400g) for this recipe.

sweet muffins

Savoury Muffins

Carrot & courgette muffins

preparation time 10 minutes **cooking time** 20 minutes **makes** 12

2 cups (300g) self-raising flour

½ cup (110g) firmly packed brown sugar

1 teaspoon ground cumin

½ teaspoon bicarbonate of soda

1 cup (110g) lightly packed, coarsely grated carrot

1 cup (110g) lightly packed, coarsely grated courgette

½ cup (60g) coarsely grated cheddar cheese

2 eggs

¾ cup (180ml) buttermilk

90g butter, melted

1 Preheat oven to 200ºC/180ºC fan-assisted. Line 12-hole (80ml) muffin pan with paper cases.

2 Sift flour, sugar, cumin and soda into large bowl; stir in carrot, courgette and cheese then eggs, buttermilk and butter. Do not over-mix; mixture should be lumpy.

3 Drop ¼ cups of mixture into paper cases; bake about 20 minutes. Stand muffins in pan 5 minutes before turning, top-side up, onto wire rack to cool.

Roasted pepper & feta muffins

preparation time 15 minutes cooking time 30 minutes makes 6

1 medium (200g) red pepper

1 medium (200g) yellow pepper

2½ cups (375g) self-raising flour

100g feta cheese, chopped

½ cup (40g) grated fresh parmesan cheese

90g butter, melted

1 egg, lightly beaten

1 cup (250ml) milk

1 tablespoon chopped fresh rosemary

½ teaspoon ground black pepper

1 tablespoon sesame seeds

1 Preheat oven to 200°C/180°C fan-assisted. Line 6-hole large (180ml) muffin pan with paper cases.

2 Quarter peppers, remove seeds and membranes. Grill or roast both peppers, skin side up, until skin blisters and blackens. Peel skin away, roughly chop flesh.

3 Sift flour into large bowl, stir in peppers, cheeses, butter, egg, milk, rosemary and black pepper.

4 Spoon mixture into prepared pan, sprinkle with seeds. Bake about 30 minutes. Stand muffins 5 minutes before turning, top-side up, onto wire rack to cool.

Peppered courgette & leek muffins

preparation time 15 minutes cooking time 20 minutes makes 12

1 tablespoon olive oil

1 medium (350g) leek, sliced

3 small (270g) courgettes, grated

2 cloves garlic, crushed

2 cups (300g) self-raising flour

2 teaspoons curry powder

1 teaspoon ground coriander

1 teaspoon ground cumin

100g butter, chopped

½ cup (60g) grated cheddar cheese

2 eggs, lightly beaten

1 cup (250ml) buttermilk

2 tablespoons olive oil, extra

TOPPING

¾ cup (90g) grated cheddar cheese

1 teaspoon cracked black pepper

1 teaspoon sea salt

1 Preheat oven to 200°C/180°C fan-assisted. Grease 12-hole (80ml) muffin pan.

2 Heat oil in medium pan, add leek, courgettes and garlic, cook, stirring, until leek is soft and any liquid evaporated. Strain mixture, press out excess liquid; cool.

3 Sift flour, curry powder and spices into large bowl, rub in butter, stir in courgette mixture and cheese, then eggs, buttermilk and extra oil.

4 Spoon mixture into prepared pan, sprinkle with topping. Bake about 20 minutes. Stand muffins 5 minutes before turning, top-side up, onto wire rack to cool.

TOPPING Combine all ingredients in small bowl; mix well.

Polenta & cottage cheese muffins

preparation time 20 minutes **cooking time** 20 minutes **makes** 12

2 cups (300g) self-raising flour

2 teaspoons caster sugar

½ cup (85g) polenta

250g low-fat cottage cheese

⅓ cup (25g) coarsely grated parmesan cheese

½ teaspoon dried chilli flakes

4 spring onions, chopped finely

1 egg

1 cup (250ml) skimmed milk

2 tablespoons vegetable oil

1 Preheat oven to 200°C/180°C fan-assisted. Grease 12-hole (80ml) muffin pan.

2 Combine flour, sugar and ⅓ cup of the polenta in medium bowl with cottage cheese, parmesan, chilli and onion. Stir in combined egg, milk and oil. Divide mixture among prepared holes of muffin pan; sprinkle with remaining polenta.

3 Bake, uncovered, about 20 minutes. Stand muffins in pan 5 minutes; turn onto wire rack to cool.

Polenta is a flour-like cereal made of ground corn. A staple in many cuisines, it is eaten in many different ways: North Americans (who call it cornmeal) eat it for breakfast doused in maple syrup; Mexicans use it as the basis for sweet tamales; and Italians use it in biscuits and cakes. It comes in both white and yellow corn varieties, and can be found ground in various textures.

Asparagus, salmon & mustard muffins

preparation time 15 minutes cooking time 20 minutes makes 12

200g fresh asparagus

2½ cups (375g) self-raising flour

2 eggs, lightly beaten

1 cup (250ml) buttermilk

2 tablespoons dijon mustard

125g butter, melted

100g smoked salmon, finely chopped

TOPPING

30g butter

¼ cup (40g) chopped almonds

1 tablespoon finely grated parmesan cheese

1 teaspoon drained green peppercorns, crushed

1 Preheat oven to 200°C/180°C fan-assisted. Grease 12-hole (80ml) muffin pan.

2 Snap off and discard tough ends of asparagus. Boil, steam or microwave asparagus until just tender. Drain, rinse under cold water, drain on kitchen paper; cool. Chop asparagus roughly.

3 Sift flour into large bowl, stir in eggs, buttermilk, mustard and butter, then asparagus and salmon.

4 Spoon mixture into prepared pan, sprinkle with topping. Bake in about 20 minutes. Stand muffins in pan 5 minutes; turn onto wire rack to cool.

TOPPING Melt butter in small pan, add nuts, stir over heat until just beginning to brown. Stir in cheese and peppercorns.

Chickpea & spinach muffins

preparation time 20 minutes cooking time 25 minutes makes 6

1/4 cup (40g) cornmeal

1 tablespoon vegetable oil

4 spring onions, chopped

2 cloves garlic, crushed

40 leaves spinach, shredded

2 cups (300g) self-raising flour

1 cup (170g) cornmeal, extra

2 tablespoons finely chopped fresh basil leaves

1 egg, lightly beaten

1¼ cups (310ml) milk

90g butter, melted

300g can chickpeas, rinsed, drained

2 tablespoons finely grated parmesan cheese

1 Preheat oven to 200°C/180°C fan-assisted. Grease 6-hole large (180ml) muffin pan. Sprinkle inside of trays with about half the cornmeal.

2 Heat oil in medium pan, add onion and garlic, cook, stirring, until onion is just soft. Add spinach, cook, stirring, until spinach is just wilted; cool.

3 Sift flour and extra cornmeal into large bowl, stir in basil, egg, milk and butter, then spinach mixture and chickpeas.

4 Spoon mixture into prepared pan, sprinkle with cheese and remaining cornmeal. Bake about 25 minutes. Stand muffins in pan 5 minutes; turn onto wire rack to cool.

savoury muffins

Mini cheesy muffins

preparation time 10 minutes **cooking time** 25 minutes **makes** 12

3 cups (450g) self-raising flour

40g butter, chopped coarsely

1¾ cups (430ml) buttermilk

2 tablespoons basil pesto

¾ cup (90g) coarsely grated cheddar cheese

¼ teaspoon sweet paprika

1 tablespoon plain flour

1 Preheat oven to 200°C/180°C fan-assisted. Grease 12-hole (80ml) muffin pan.

2 Place self-raising flour in large bowl; rub in butter with fingertips. Using fork, stir in buttermilk to form a soft, sticky dough. Swirl pesto and cheese through; do not overmix.

3 Divide mixture among holes of prepared pan. Sprinkle with combined paprika and plain flour.

4 Bake about 25 minutes. Stand muffins in pan 5 minutes before turning out onto wire rack to cool.

tip You can make your own pesto, but we used bottled pesto to save time. A sun-dried tomato pesto can also be used.

Savoury muffins make great snacks and should be quite distinct in flavour. Use a strong, mature cheese for best results and season the mixtures with salt and pepper to make sure they taste good after they're baked. The muffins in this chapter make great lunchbox fillers, handy picnic fare or tasty accompaniments to soup on a cold winter's night.

Prosciutto, basil & tomato muffins

preparation time 15 minutes **cooking time** 30 minutes **makes** 6

5 slices (75g) prosciutto

2½ cups (375g) self-raising flour

90g butter

1 egg, lightly beaten

1¼ cups (310ml) buttermilk

⅓ cup (80ml) milk

⅓ cup (50g) drained chopped sun-dried tomatoes

2 tablespoons chopped fresh basil leaves

1 clove garlic, crushed

1 teaspoon cracked black pepper

1 tablespoon olive oil

1 Preheat oven to 200°C/180°C fan-assisted. Grease 6-hole (180ml) muffin pan. Cut prosciutto into strips.

2 Sift flour into large bowl, rub in butter, stir in egg, buttermilk, milk, tomatoes, basil, garlic and pepper.

3 Spoon mixture into prepared pan, top with prosciutto, brush lightly with oil. Bake muffins about 20 minutes. Cover with foil, bake a further 10 minutes. Stand muffins in pan 5 minutes; turn onto wire rack to cool.

Crusty cheese & onion muffins

preparation time 15 minutes **cooking time** 25 minutes **makes** 6

¼ cup (35g) plain flour

20g butter

1 teaspoon water, approximately

1 tablespoon vegetable oil

1 medium (150g) onion, halved, sliced

1¾ cups (260g) self-raising flour

¾ cup (110g) plain flour, extra

¾ cup (90g) grated cheddar cheese

1 tablespoon chopped fresh chives

1 egg, lightly beaten

1¼ cups (310ml) buttermilk

½ cup (125ml) vegetable oil, extra

CHIVE BUTTER

40g cream cheese, softened

50g butter, softened

2 teaspoons lemon juice

1 tablespoon chopped fresh chives

1 Place plain flour in small bowl, rub in butter, mix in just enough water to bind ingredients. Press dough into a ball, cover, freeze about 30 minutes or until firm.

2 Preheat oven to 200°C/180°C fan-assisted. Grease 6-hole (180ml) muffin pan.

3 Heat oil in frying pan, add onion, cook, stirring, until soft and lightly browned; cool.

4 Sift self-raising and extra plain flour into large bowl, stir in half the onion, half the cheese and all the chives, then egg, buttermilk and extra oil.

5 Spoon mixture into prepared pan. Grate frozen dough into small bowl, quickly mix in remaining onion and cheese; sprinkle over muffins. Bake muffins about 25 minutes. Stand muffins in pan 5 minutes; turn onto wire rack to cool. Serve with chive butter.
CHIVE BUTTER Beat cheese and butter together in a small bowl until smooth, stir in juice and chives.

Arrabbiata Muffins

Arrabbiata muffins

preparation time 20 minutes **cooking time** 20 minutes **makes** 12

120g pancetta, finely chopped

2 cups (300g) self-raising flour

1 cup (150g) plain flour

⅓ cup (25g) coarsely grated fresh parmesan cheese

¾ cup (90g) pitted sliced black olives

2 tablespoons shredded fresh basil leaves

1 tablespoon chopped fresh oregano

2 eggs, lightly beaten

2 tablespoons tomato purée

3 teaspoons sambal oelek

3 cloves garlic, crushed

¾ cup (180ml) vegetable oil

1½ cups (375ml) buttermilk

1 tablespoon shredded fresh basil leaves, extra

1 Preheat oven to 200°C/180°C fan-assisted. Grease 12-hole (80ml) muffin pan.

2 Cook bacon in heated pan until crisp, drain on absorbent paper, allow to cool.

3 Sift flours into large bowl, stir in bacon, cheese, olives and herbs, then eggs, purée, sambal oelek, garlic, oil and buttermilk.

4 Spoon mixture into prepared pan, sprinkle with extra basil. Bake muffins about 20 minutes. Stand muffins in pan 5 minutes; turn onto wire rack to cool.

Pancetta is an Italian salt-cured pork roll, usually cut from the belly. Finely sliced, it is usually used, chopped, in cooked dishes to add flavours. If you prefer, thinly sliced bacon can be substituted. Sambal oelek is a salty paste made from ground chillies. It can be very hot, so use it sparingly.

savoury muffins

Ham & cheese muffins

preparation time 15 minutes **cooking time** 20 minutes **makes** 12

2 cups (300g) self-raising flour

½ teaspoon chicken stock powder

½ teaspoon ground hot paprika

80g butter

6 slices (130g) ham, chopped

1½ cups (185g) coarsely grated cheddar cheese

1 egg, lightly beaten

1 cup (250ml) milk

ground hot paprika, extra

1 Preheat oven to 200°C/180°C fan-assisted. Grease 12-hole (80ml) muffin pan.

2 Sift dry ingredients into large bowl, rub in butter. Stir in ham and cheese, then egg and milk.

3 Spoon mixture into prepared pan, sprinkle with a little extra paprika. Bake muffins about 20 minutes. Stand muffins in pan 5 minutes; turn onto wire rack to cool.

Bacon & fresh herb muffins

preparation time 15 minutes **cooking time** 25 minutes (plus cooling time) **makes** 12

6 bacon rashers, chopped finely

3 cups (450g) self-raising flour

60g butter, chopped coarsely

1 tablespoon coarsely chopped fresh basil

2 tablespoons coarsely chopped fresh chives

2 teaspoons coarsely chopped fresh oregano

¾ cup (60g) grated parmesan cheese

2 eggs, beaten lightly

1 cup (250ml) milk

1 Preheat oven to 200°C/180°C fan-assisted. Grease 12-hole (80ml) muffin pan.

2 Cook bacon in small frying pan until crisp. Drain on absorbent paper; cool.

3 Place flour in large bowl; rub in butter. Add bacon, herbs and cheese, then combined eggs and milk. Mix using fork until ingredients are just combined; do not over-mix. Mixture should be coarse and lumpy.

4 Spoon mixture into prepared pan; bake about 20 minutes. Stand muffins in pan 5 minutes; turn onto wire rack to cool.

Cheese, corn & bacon muffins

preparation time 25 minutes **cooking time** 20 minutes (plus standing time) **makes** 12

½ cup (85g) polenta

½ cup (125ml) milk

3 bacon rashers (210g), rind removed, chopped finely

4 spring onions, chopped finely

1½ cups (225g) self-raising flour

1 tablespoon caster sugar

310g can corn kernels, drained

125g can creamed corn

100g butter, melted

2 eggs, beaten lightly

50g piece cheddar cheese

¼ cup (30g) coarsely grated cheddar cheese

1 Preheat oven to 180°C/160°C fan-assisted. Grease 12-hole (80ml) muffin pan.

2 Mix polenta and milk in small bowl, cover; stand 20 minutes.

3 Meanwhile, cook bacon, stirring, in heated small frying pan for 2 minutes. Add onion to pan; cook, stirring, for another 2 minutes. Remove pan from heat; cool 5 minutes.

4 Sift flour and sugar into large bowl; stir in corn kernels, creamed corn and bacon mixture. Add melted butter, eggs and polenta mixture; mix muffin batter only until just combined.

5 Spoon 1 tablespoon of the batter into each hole of muffin pan. Cut piece of cheese into 12 equal pieces; place one piece in the centre of each muffin tin hole. Divide remaining batter among tin holes; sprinkle grated cheese over each.

6 Bake muffins about 20 minutes. Stand in pan 5 minutes; turn onto wire rack. Serve muffins warm.

If you like to eat your muffins with butter, create your own complementary flavoured butter. Bring butter to room temperature and beat in a small quantity of the flavouring – chilli, lemon & parsley (dried chilli flakes, finely grated lemon rind and finely chopped flat-leaf parsley), mustard and tarragon (wholegrain mustard and finely chopped fresh tarragon), or try one of the flavours suggested on page 5.

savoury muffins

72

Pear, pecan & blue cheese muffins

preparation time 15 minutes **cooking time** 20 minutes **makes** 12

2½ cups (375g) self-raising flour

1 cup (125g) chopped pecans

1 teaspoon cracked black pepper

150g soft blue cheese, chopped

425g can pear halves in light syrup, drained, chopped

2 eggs, lightly beaten

½ cup (125ml) vegetable oil

½ cup (125ml) milk

1 Preheat oven to 180°C/160°C fan-assisted. Grease 12-hole (80ml) muffin pan.
2 Sift flour into large bowl, stir in nuts, pepper, cheese and pear, then eggs, oil and milk.
3 Spoon mixture into prepared pan, sprinkle with extra cracked pepper. Bake about 20 minutes. Stand muffins in pan 5 minutes; turn onto wire rack to cool.

Cranberry & camembert muffins

preparation time 15 minutes **cooking time** 20 minutes **makes** 12

2 cups (300g) self-raising flour

2 tablespoons caster sugar

2 eggs, lightly beaten

⅓ cup (80ml) cranberry sauce

125g camembert cheese, finely chopped

½ cup plain yogurt

¼ cup (60ml) milk

60g butter, melted

½ cup (125ml) cranberry sauce, extra

⅓ cup (40g) chopped walnuts

1 Preheat oven to 180°C/160°C fan-assisted. Grease 12-hole (80ml) muffin pan.
2 Sift dry ingredients into large bowl, stir in eggs, sauce, cheese, yogurt, milk and butter.
3 Half-fill prepared pan with mixture, make a well in each muffin, drop rounded teaspoons of extra sauce into each well, top with remaining muffin mixture. Sprinkle with nuts. Bake about 20 minutes. Stand muffins in pan 5 minutes; turn onto wire rack to cool.

savoury muffins

Triple-cheese muffins

preparation time 10 minutes cooking time 20 minutes makes 8

1 cup (150g) self-raising flour

½ teaspoon bicarbonate of soda

¼ teaspoon cayenne pepper

2 eggs

1¼ cups (310ml) milk

20g butter, melted

4 spring onions, chopped finely

2 tablespoons finely grated mozzarella cheese

2 tablespoons finely grated parmesan cheese

2 tablespoons finely grated cheddar cheese

1 Preheat oven to 200°C/180°C fan-assisted. Grease eight holes of 12-hole (80ml) muffin pan.

2 Sift flour, soda and cayenne into medium bowl. Whisk egg, milk, butter and onion in small bowl. Pour egg mixture into flour mixture; whisk until combined. Do not over-mix.

3 Spoon half of the mixture into pan holes; sprinkle with combined cheeses. Top with remaining batter.

4 Bake muffins about 20 minutes. Stand muffins in pan 5 minutes; turn, top-side up, onto wire rack to cool.

Both mozzarella and parmesan are Italian cheeses. Originally made from buffalo's milk but now also from cow's milk, mozzarella is soft and white, and keeps for 2 days in brine in the fridge. Parmesan is the king of hard cheeses. The best is Parmigiano-reggiano from the strictly defined Emilia-Romagna cheese-making region in northern Italy. Much used for grating, it is also a splendid table cheese.

Spicy chorizo & corn muffins

preparation time 20 minutes **cooking time** 25 minutes **makes** 6

1¾ cups (260g) self-raising flour

1 teaspoon dried crushed chillies

½ teaspoon ground cumin

½ teaspoon ground coriander

1 teaspoon ground hot paprika

¾ cup (90g) coarsely grated smoked cheese

90g chorizo, chopped

½ medium (100g) red pepper, chopped

½ medium (100g) green pepper, chopped

1 clove garlic, crushed

1 small (80g) onion, grated

130g can creamed corn

2 eggs, lightly beaten

90g butter, melted

1 cup (250ml) buttermilk

½ teaspoon ground hot paprika, extra

1 Preheat oven to 200°C/180°C fan-assisted. Grease 6-hole large (180ml) muffin pan.
2 Sift flour into large bowl, add chillies, spices, cheese, chorizo and peppers; mix well. Add garlic, onion and corn, then stir in eggs, butter and buttermilk.
3 Spoon mixture into prepared pan, sprinkle with extra paprika. Bake about 25 minutes. Stand muffins in pan 5 minutes; turn onto wire rack to cool.

Caramelised onion & polenta muffins

preparation time 15 minutes **cooking time** 20 minutes **makes** 12

2 tablespoons olive oil

3 medium (450g) onions, sliced

1 teaspoon cumin seeds

1 teaspoon dried crushed chillies

2 tablespoons white vinegar

2 tablespoons caster sugar

3 cups (450g) self-raising flour

2 cups (340g) polenta

2 eggs, lightly beaten

185g butter, melted

1⅓ cups (330ml) milk

¼ cup chopped fresh parsley

1 tablespoon chopped fresh thyme

1 Preheat oven to 200°C/180°C fan-assisted. Grease 12-hole (80ml) muffin pan.
2 Heat oil in pan, add onions, seeds and chillies, cook, stirring, until onions are soft. Add vinegar and sugar, cook, stirring occasionally, about 20 minutes or until onions are golden brown; cool. Reserve ¼ cup onion mixture.
3 Sift flour into large bowl, stir in onion mixture with remaining ingredients.
4 Spoon mixture into prepared pan. Bake about 20 minutes. Stand muffins in pan 5 minutes; turn onto wire rack to cool. Serve muffins topped with reserved onion mixture.

savoury muffins

Cheesy pizza muffins

preparation time 15 minutes   **cooking time** 25 minutes   **makes** 6

1 small (150g) red pepper

2½ cups (375g) self-raising flour

1 egg, lightly beaten

1¼ cups (310ml) milk

⅓ cup (80ml) light olive oil

½ cup (60g) grated cheddar cheese

¼ cup (20g) grated fresh parmesan cheese

½ cup (60g) pitted black olives, halved

¼ cup (35g) drained chopped
sun-dried tomatoes

2 tablespoons chopped fresh basil leaves

2 teaspoons chopped fresh rosemary

¼ cup (30g) grated cheddar cheese, extra

1   Preheat oven to 200°C/180°C fan-assisted. Grease 6-hole large (180ml) muffin pan.

2   Quarter pepper, remove seeds and membranes. Grill pepper, skin side up, until skin blisters and blackens. Peel skin away, cut flesh into strips.

3   Sift flour into large bowl, stir in egg, milk, oil, cheeses, olives, tomatoes and herbs.

3   Spoon mixture into prepared pan, top with pepper strips, sprinkle with extra cheese. Bake about 25 minutes. Stand muffins in pan 5 minutes; turn onto wire rack to cool.

Curried chicken muffins

preparation time 15 minutes   cooking time 20 minutes   **makes** 12

1 tablespoon vegetable oil

1 small (80g) onion, finely chopped

3 (330g) chicken thigh fillets, finely chopped

2 tablespoons Madras curry paste

1 cup (250ml) plain yogurt

2¼ cups (335g) self-raising flour

½ cup (125ml) vegetable oil, extra

2 eggs, lightly beaten

2 tablespoons lemon juice

2 tablespoons chopped fresh coriander leaves

ground hot paprika

1   Preheat oven to 200°C/180°C fan-assisted. Grease 12-hole (80ml) muffin pan.

2   Heat oil in pan, add onion, cook, stirring, until onion is soft. Add chicken, cook, stirring, until chicken is just tender. Stir in curry paste, remove from heat, stir in yogurt; cool.

3   Sift flour into large bowl, stir in chicken mixture, extra oil, eggs, juice and coriander.

4   Spoon mixture into prepared pan, sprinkle with a little paprika. Bake about 20 minutes. Stand muffins in pan 5 minutes; turn onto wire rack to cool.

savoury muffins

Cream cheese, corn & sweet chilli muffins

preparation time 10 minutes (plus standing time) **cooking time** 20 minutes **makes** 12

½ cup (85g) polenta

1 cup (250ml) buttermilk

40g butter, melted

2 eggs, beaten lightly

⅓ cup (80ml) sweet chilli sauce

1 medium brown onion (150g), chopped finely

1½ cups (225g) self-raising flour

310g can corn kernels, drained

125g packet reduced-fat cream cheese

1 Preheat oven to 200°C/180°C fan-assisted. Grease 12-hole (80ml) muffin pan.

2 Mix polenta and buttermilk in small bowl; stand 20 minutes. Stir in butter, egg and two tablespoons of the sauce.

3 Meanwhile, cook onion in heated small frying pan, stirring, about 5 minutes or until onion softens. Cool 5 minutes.

4 Combine onion, flour and kernels in medium bowl. Add polenta mixture; mix batter until combined.

5 Spoon 1 tablespoon batter into each pan hole. Cut cheese into 12 equal pieces; place one piece into batter in pan then cover each with remaining batter, drizzle with remaining sauce.

6 Bake about 20 minutes. Stand muffins in pan 5 minutes; turn onto wire rack. Serve muffins warm.

tip Reheat leftover muffins in a microwave oven on HIGH (100%) for 20 seconds each.

Cheesy sweet potato muffins

preparation time 15 minutes **cooking time** 30 minutes **makes** 12

2 cups (300g) self-raising flour, sifted

1 cup (180G) grated sweet potato, firmly packed

2 tablespoons snipped chives

²⁄₃ cup (165ml) buttermilk

125g butter, melted

1 egg, lightly beaten

125g cheddar cheese, cut into 12 cubes

1 Preheat oven to 200°C/180°C fan-assisted. Grease 12-hole (80ml) muffin pan.

2 Combine flour, sweet potato and half the chives in a medium bowl. Add buttermilk, butter and egg.

3 Spoon into the prepared pan. Press a cube of cheese into each. Sprinkle with remaining chives. Bake for 25-30 minutes. Stand muffins in pan 5 minutes; turn onto wire rack.

Cheese, ham & pineapple muffins

preparation time 15 minutes **cooking time** 25 minutes **makes** 12

2 cups (300g) self-raising flour, sifted

1 cup (120g) grated cheddar cheese

100g sliced ham, chopped

4 pineapple rings, chopped

3 tablespoons chopped fresh parsley

²⁄₃ cup (165ml) milk

125g butter, melted, cooled

1 egg, lightly beaten

1 Preheat oven to 200°C/180°C fan-assisted. Grease 12-hole (80ml) muffin pan.

2 Combine flour, cheese, ham, pineapple and parsley in a medium bowl. Add milk, butter and egg.

3 Spoon into the prepared pan. Bake for 20-25 minutes. Stand muffins in pan 5 minutes; turn onto wire rack. Serve muffins warm.

savoury muffins

Madeleines & Morsels

Madeleines

preparation time 15 minutes **cooking time** 10 minutes **makes** 24

2 eggs

2 tablespoons caster sugar

2 tablespoons icing sugar

¼ cup (35g) self-raising flour

¼ cup (35g) plain flour

75g unsalted butter, melted

1 tablespoon water

2 tablespoons icing sugar, extra

1 Preheat oven to 200°C/180°C fan-assisted. Grease two 12-hole (30ml) madeleine pans.

2 Beat eggs and sifted sugars in small bowl with electric mixer until thick and creamy.

3 Meanwhile, triple-sift flours; sift flour over egg mixture. Pour combined butter and the water down side of bowl then fold ingredients together.

4 Drop rounded tablespoons of mixture into each pan hole. Bake about 10 minutes. Tap hot pan firmly on worktop to release madeleines then turn, top-side down, onto wire rack to cool. Serve dusted with sifted extra icing sugar.

Orange madeleines

preparation time 15 minutes **cooking time** 10 minutes **makes** 24

2 eggs

2 tablespoons caster sugar

2 tablespoons icing sugar

1 teaspoon finely grated orange rind

1 teaspoon vanilla extract

¼ cup (35g) self-raising flour

¼ cup (35g) plain flour

75g butter, melted

1 tablespoon orange juice.

2 tablespoons icing sugar, extra

1 Preheat oven to 180°C/160°C fan-assisted. Grease two 12-hole (30ml) madeleine pans with a little butter.

2 Beat eggs, caster sugar, icing sugar, rind and extract in small bowl with electric mixer until thick and creamy.

3 Meanwhile, sift flours twice. Sift flours over egg mixture; pour combined butter and orange juice down side of bowl then fold ingredients together.

4 Drop rounded tablespoons of mixture into pan holes.

5 Bake madeleines about 10 minutes. Tap hot pan firmly on worktop to release madeleines then turn immediately onto baking-parchment-covered wire racks to cool. Serve dusted with extra sifted icing sugar.

Lemon madeleines

preparation time 15 minutes **cooking time** 10 minutes **makes** 12

2 eggs

2 tablespoons caster sugar

2 tablespoons icing sugar

2 teaspoons finely grated lemon rind

¼ cup (35g) self-raising flour

¼ cup (35g) plain flour

75g unsalted butter, melted

1 tablespoon lemon juice

2 tablespoons icing sugar, extra

1 Preheat oven to 200°C/180°C fan-assisted. Grease 12-hole (30ml) madeleine tin.

2 Beat eggs, caster sugar, sifted icing sugar and rind in small bowl with electric mixer until pale and thick.

3 Meanwhile, triple-sift flours; sift flour over egg mixture. Pour butter and juice down the side of the bowl then fold ingredients together.

4 Drop rounded tablespoons of mixture into each hole of tin. Bake about 10 minutes. Tap hot tin firmly on worktop to release madeleines onto wire rack to cool.

5 Dust with sifted extra icing sugar to serve.

Golden pecan twists

preparation time 25 minutes **cooking time** 10 minutes **makes** 30

2 tablespoons golden syrup

⅓ cup (40g) finely chopped pecans

125g butter, softened

¼ teaspoon vanilla extract

⅓ cup (75g) caster sugar

1 egg yolk

1 cup (150g) plain flour

1 Preheat oven to 180°C/160°C fan-assisted. Grease oven trays; line with baking parchment.

2 Combine half of the golden syrup with nuts in small bowl.

3 Beat butter, extract, sugar, remaining golden syrup and egg yolk in small bowl with electric mixer until light and fluffy. Stir in sifted flour.

4 Shape rounded teaspoons of mixture into balls; roll each ball into 12cm log. Twist each log into a loop, overlapping one end over the other. Place twists on trays 3cm apart; top each twist with ½ teaspoon nut mixture.

5 Bake twists about 10 minutes; cool twists on trays.

Coconut French macaroons

preparation time 25 minutes **cooking time** 20 minutes (plus standing time) **makes** 16

3 egg whites

¼ cup (55g) caster sugar

½ teaspoon coconut essence

1¼ cups (200g) icing sugar

¾ cup (90g) ground almonds

¼ cup (20g) desiccated coconut

1 tablespoon icing sugar, extra

WHITE CHOCOLATE GANACHE

¼ cup (60ml) single cream

155g white eating chocolate, chopped coarsely

2 teaspoons coconut-flavoured liqueur

1 Preheat oven to 130°C/110°C fan-assisted. Grease oven trays; line with baking parchment.

2 Beat egg whites in small bowl with electric mixer until soft peaks form. Add caster sugar and essence, beat until sugar dissolves; transfer mixture to large bowl. Fold in sifted icing sugar, ground almonds and coconut, in two batches.

3 Spoon mixture into piping bag fitted with 1cm plain tube. Pipe 4cm rounds about 2.5cm apart onto trays. Tap trays on bench so macaroons spread slightly. Stand 30 minutes.

4 Bake macaroons about 20 minutes. Cool on trays.

5 Meanwhile, make white chocolate ganache.

6 Sandwich macaroons with ganache. Serve dusted with extra sifted icing sugar.
   WHITE CHOCOLATE GANACHE Bring cream to the boil in small saucepan. Remove from heat; pour over chocolate in small bowl, stir until smooth. Stir in liqueur. Stand at room temperature until spreadable.

Hazelnut pinwheels

preparation time 20 minutes (plus refrigeration time) **baking time** 20 minutes **makes** 30

1¼ cups (185g) plain flour

100g butter, chopped

½ cup (110g) caster sugar

1 egg yolk

1 tablespoon milk, approximately

⅓ cup (110g) chocolate hazelnut spread

2 tablespoons ground hazelnuts

1 Process flour, butter and sugar until crumbly. Add egg yolk; process with enough milk until mixture forms a ball. Knead dough on lightly floured surface until smooth; cover, refrigerate 1 hour.

2 Roll dough between sheets of baking parchment to form 20cm x 30cm rectangle; remove top sheet of paper. Spread dough evenly with hazelnut spread; sprinkle with ground hazelnuts. Using paper as a guide, roll dough tightly from long side to enclose filling. Enclose roll in cling film; refrigerate 30 minutes.

3 Preheat oven to 180°C/160°C fan-assisted. Grease oven trays; line with baking parchment.

4 Remove film from dough; cut roll into 1cm slices. Place slices on trays 2cm apart. Bake about 20 minutes. Stand pinwheels on trays 5 minutes; transfer to wire rack to cool.

If you don't have ground hazelnuts in your pantry, it's easy enough to grind the nuts yourself for the small amount required here. Toast the nuts briefly in a small frying pan, stirring constantly to ensure they don't burn. Cool then wrap in a tea-towel and rub off their skins. Process in a coffee- or spice-grinder (or mini food processor) to a coarse flour consistency. Take care – too long and they'll turn into an oily paste.

Gingernuts

preparation time 15 minutes (plus cooling time) **cooking time** 10 minutes **makes** 32

90g butter

⅓ cup (75g) firmly packed brown sugar

⅓ cup (115g) golden syrup

1⅓ cups (200g) plain flour

¾ teaspoon bicarbonate of soda

1 tablespoon ground ginger

1 teaspoon ground cinnamon

¼ teaspoon ground cloves

1 Preheat oven to 180°C/160°C fan-assisted. Grease oven trays.

2 Combine butter, sugar and syrup in medium saucepan; stir over low heat until smooth. Remove from heat; stir in sifted dry ingredients. Cool 10 minutes.

3 Roll rounded teaspoons of mixture into balls. Place about 3cm apart on trays; flatten slightly. Bake about 10 minutes; cool on trays.

Vanilla bean thins

preparation time 20 minutes **cooking time** 5 minutes **makes** 24

1 vanilla pod

30g butter, softened

¼ cup (55g) caster sugar

1 egg white, beaten lightly

¼ cup (35g) plain flour

1 Preheat oven to 200°C/180°C fan-assisted. Grease oven trays; line with baking parchment.

2 Halve vanilla pod lengthways; scrape seeds into medium bowl with butter and sugar, discard pod. Stir until combined, stir in egg white and flour. Spoon mixture into piping bag fitted with 5mm plain nozzle.

3 Pipe 6cm-long strips (making them slightly wider at both ends) 5cm apart on trays. Bake about 5 minutes or until edges are browned lightly; cool biscuits on trays.

Vanilla kisses

preparation time 15 minutes **cooking time** 10 minutes **makes** 20

125g butter, softened

½ cup (110g) caster sugar

1 egg

⅓ cup (50g) plain flour

¼ cup (35g) self-raising flour

⅔ cup (100g) cornflour

¼ cup (30g) custard powder

VIENNA CREAM

60g butter, softened

½ teaspoon vanilla extract

¾ cup (120g) icing sugar

2 teaspoons milk

1 Preheat oven to 200°C/180°C fan-assisted. Grease oven trays; line with baking parchment.

2 Beat butter, sugar and egg in small bowl with electric mixer until light and fluffy. Stir in sifted dry ingredients, in two batches.

3 Spoon mixture into piping bag fitted with 1cm-fluted nozzle. Pipe 3cm rosettes about 3cm apart on trays. Bake about 10 minutes; cool on trays.

4 Meanwhile, make vienna cream. Sandwich biscuits with vienna cream.
   VIENNA CREAM Beat butter and extract in small bowl with electric mixer until as white as possible; gradually beat in sifted icing sugar and milk, in two batches.

Chocolate melting moments

preparation time 15 minutes **cooking time** 10 minutes **makes** 20

125g butter, softened

2 tablespoons icing sugar

¾ cup (110g) plain flour

2 tablespoons cornflour

1 tablespoon cocoa powder

¼ cup (85g) chocolate hazelnut spread

1 Preheat oven to 180°C/160°C fan-assisted. Grease oven trays; line with baking parchment.

2 Beat butter and sifted icing sugar in small bowl with electric mixer until light and fluffy. Stir in sifted dry ingredients.

3 Spoon mixture into piping bag fitted with 1cm-fluted nozzle. Pipe stars about 3cm apart on trays. Bake about 10 minutes; cool on trays. Sandwich biscuits with hazelnut spread.

madeleines & morsels

Amanda Tunic

wild floral print chiffon

adam drawstring pant

crop lace top

Victorian cami

Katie top

Coffee meringue kisses

preparation time 15 minutes **cooking time** 30 minutes **makes** 45

¾ cup (165g) caster sugar

1 teaspoon instant coffee granules

¼ cup (60ml) water

1 egg white

1 teaspoon malt vinegar

2 teaspoons cornflour

COFFEE BUTTER CREAM

1 teaspoon instant coffee granules

2 teaspoons hot water

2 teaspoons coffee-flavoured liqueur

60g unsalted butter, softened

⅔ cup (110g) icing sugar

1 Preheat oven to 120°C/100°C fan-assisted. Grease four oven trays; line with baking parchment.

2 Combine sugar, coffee and the water in small saucepan; stir over heat until sugar is dissolved. Bring to a boil; remove pan from heat.

3 Meanwhile, combine egg white, vinegar and cornflour in small heatproof bowl; beat with electric mixer until foamy. With motor operating, add hot syrup to egg white in a thin, steady stream; beat about 10 minutes or until mixture is thick.

4 Spoon meringue into piping bag fitted with 5mm-fluted nozzle; pipe meringues, about 2.5cm in diameter, about 3cm apart, on trays. Bake about 30 minutes or until dry to touch. Cool on trays.

5 Meanwhile, make coffee butter cream. Sandwich meringues with butter cream just before serving.
   COFFEE BUTTER CREAM Dissolve coffee in the water; add liqueur. Beat butter and sifted icing sugar until light and fluffy; beat in coffee mixture.

Use dry, grease-free utensils to beat room temperature egg whites, watching carefully for the forming of 'soft' peaks, those that literally fall over when the beaters are lifted. Beating the mixture any longer is likely to make it so dry that the sugar won't dissolve.

madeleines & morsels

Orange hazelnut butter yoyo bites

preparation time 15 minutes **cooking time** 15 minutes **makes** 20

250g unsalted butter, softened

1 teaspoon vanilla extract

½ cup (80g) icing sugar

1½ cups (225g) plain flour

½ cup (75g) cornflour

ORANGE HAZELNUT BUTTER CREAM

80g unsalted butter, softened

2 teaspoons finely grated orange rind

⅔ cup (110g) icing sugar

1 tablespoon ground hazelnuts

1 Preheat oven to 160°C/140°C fan-assisted. Grease oven trays; line with baking parchment.

2 Beat butter, extract and sifted icing sugar in small bowl with electric mixer until light and fluffy; stir in sifted dry ingredients, in two batches.

3 Roll rounded teaspoons of mixture into balls; place about 3cm apart on trays. Using fork dusted with flour, press tines gently onto each biscuit to flatten slightly. Bake about 15 minutes; cool on trays.

4 Meanwhile, make orange hazelnut butter cream.

5 Sandwich biscuits with orange hazelnut butter cream; dust with extra sifted icing sugar, if desired.

ORANGE HAZELNUT BUTTER CREAM Beat butter, rind and sifted icing sugar in small bowl with electric mixer until light and fluffy. Stir in ground hazelnuts.

Passionfruit cream biscuits

preparation time 35 minutes (plus refrigeration and cooling time) **cooking time** 10 minutes **makes** 25

125g butter, softened

2 teaspoons finely grated lemon rind

⅓ cup (75g) caster sugar

2 tablespoons golden syrup

1 cup (150g) self-raising flour

⅔ cup (100g) plain flour

¼ cup (60ml) passionfruit pulp

PASSIONFRUIT CREAM

2 tablespoons passionfruit pulp

90g butter, softened

1 cup (160g) icing sugar

1 Beat butter, rind and sugar in small bowl with electric mixer until light and fluffy. Add golden syrup, beat until combined. Stir in sifted dry ingredients and passionfruit pulp.

2 Turn dough onto floured surface, knead gently until smooth. Cut dough in half; roll each portion between sheets of baking parchment to 5mm thickness. Refrigerate 30 minutes.

3 Preheat oven to 160°C/140°C fan-assisted. Grease oven trays; line with baking parchment.

4 Cut 25 x 4cm fluted rounds from each portion of dough; place about 2.5cm apart on trays.

5 Bake biscuits about 10 minutes. Cool on trays.

6 Meanwhile, make passionfruit cream.

7 Spoon passionfruit cream into piping bag fitted with 5mm fluted nozzle. Pipe cream onto half the biscuits; top with remaining biscuits. Serve dusted with a little extra sifted icing sugar, if you like.

PASSIONFRUIT CREAM Strain passionfruit pulp through fine sieve into small jug, discard seeds. Beat butter and sugar in small bowl with electric mixer until light and fluffy. Beat in passionfruit juice.

tip You need about 6 passionfruit for this recipe.

madeleines & morsels

Maple-syrup butter whirls

preparation time 20 minutes **cooking time** 15 minutes **makes** 24

125g butter, softened

½ teaspoon vanilla extract

⅓ cup (80ml) maple syrup

¾ cup (110g) plain flour

¼ cup (35g) cornflour

1   Preheat oven to 180°C/160°C fan-assisted. Grease oven trays; line with baking parchment.

2   Beat butter, extract and maple syrup in small bowl with electric mixer until light and fluffy; stir in combined sifted flours. Spoon mixture into piping bag fitted with 1cm fluted nozzle.

3   Pipe stars about 3cm apart onto trays. Bake about 15 minutes; cool whirls on trays.

Shortbread crescents

preparation time 35 minutes **cooking time** 15 minutes **makes** 45

250g unsalted butter, softened

1 cup (220g) caster sugar

1 egg

¼ cup (60ml) brandy

¾ cup (60g) flaked almonds, roasted, chopped finely

2½ cups (375g) plain flour

1½ cups (225g) self-raising flour

¼ cup (60ml) orange flower water

⅓ cup (80ml) water

2 cups (320g) icing sugar

1   Preheat oven to 160°C/140°C fan-assisted. Grease oven trays.

2   Beat butter and sugar in small bowl with electric mixer until light and fluffy. Add egg and brandy, beat until combined; transfer mixture to large bowl. Stir in nuts and sifted flours, in two batches.

3   Turn dough onto floured surface, knead gently until smooth. Shape level tablespoons of dough into crescent shapes; place about 2.5cm apart on trays.

4   Bake shortbread about 15 minutes. Working quickly, place shortbread onto wire racks; brush hot shortbread with combined orange flower water and the water. Toss shortbread in icing sugar; cool on wire racks.

Mini Florentines

preparation time 10 minutes (plus standing time) cooking time 5 minutes makes 25

¾ cup (120g) sultanas

2 cups (80g) corn flakes

¾ cup (60g) roasted flaked almonds

½ cup (100g) red glacé cherries

⅔ cup (160ml) sweetened condensed milk

60g white eating chocolate, melted

60g dark eating chocolate, melted

1　Preheat oven to 180°C/160°C fan-assisted. Grease oven trays; line with baking parchment.

2　Combine sultanas, corn flakes, nuts, cherries and condensed milk in medium bowl.

3　Drop level tablespoons of mixture about 5cm apart on trays. Bake for 5 minutes; cool on trays.

4　Spread half the Florentine bases with white chocolate; spread remaining half with dark chocolate. Run fork through chocolate to make waves; allow to set at room temperature.

Chocolate lace crisps

preparation time 25 minutes (plus refrigeration time) cooking time 20 minutes makes 24

100g dark cooking chocolate, chopped coarsely

80g butter, chopped

1 cup (220g) caster sugar

1 egg, beaten lightly

1 cup (150g) plain flour

2 tablespoons cocoa powder

¼ teaspoon bicarbonate of soda

¼ cup (40g) icing sugar

1　Melt chocolate and butter in small saucepan over low heat. Transfer to medium bowl.

2　Stir in caster sugar, egg and sifted flour, cocoa and bicarbonate of soda. Cover; refrigerate about 15 minutes or until mixture is firm enough to handle.

3　Preheat oven to 180°C/160°C fan-assisted. Grease oven trays; line with baking parchment.

4　Roll level tablespoons of mixture into balls; roll each ball in icing sugar, place on trays 8cm apart. Bake about 15 minutes; cool crisps on trays.

madeleines & morsels

Coconut ice cakes

preparation time 40 minutes (plus cooling time) **cooking time** 20 minutes **makes** 18

60g butter, softened

½ teaspoon coconut essence

½ cup (110g) caster sugar

1 egg

¼ cup (20g) desiccated coconut

¾ cup (110g) self-raising flour

½ cup (120g) soured cream

2 tablespoons milk

COCONUT ICE FROSTING

1 cup (160g) icing sugar

⅔ cup (50g) desiccated coconut

1 egg white, beaten lightly

pink food colouring

1 Preheat oven to 160°C/140°C fan-assisted. Line 18 holes of two 12-hole (40ml) deep flat-based muffin pans with paper cases.

2 Beat butter, essence, sugar and egg in small bowl with electric mixer until light and fluffy. Stir in the coconut, sifted flour, soured cream and milk, in two batches. Divide mixture into paper cases.

3 Bake cakes about 20 minutes. Stand cakes 5 minutes before turning top-side up onto wire rack to cool.

4 Meanwhile, make coconut ice frosting.

5 Drop alternate rounded teaspoons of white and pink frosting onto cakes; marble over the top of each cake.
   COCONUT ICE FROSTING Sift icing sugar into medium bowl; stir in coconut and egg white. Place half the mixture in small bowl; tint with pink food colouring.

tip Use a hot wet palette knife to spread the frosting over cakes.

Mini carrot cakes

preparation time 25 minutes (plus cooling time) **cooking time** 20 minutes **makes** 18

⅓ cup (80ml) vegetable oil

½ cup (110g) firmly packed light brown sugar

1 egg

1 cup firmly packed, coarsely grated carrot

⅓ cup (40g) finely chopped walnuts

¾ cup (110g) self-raising flour

½ teaspoon mixed spice

1 tablespoon pepitas, chopped finely

1 tablespoon finely chopped dried apricots

1 tablespoon finely chopped walnuts, extra

LEMON CREAM CHEESE FROSTING

90g cream cheese, softened

30g unsalted butter, softened

1 teaspoon finely grated lemon rind

1½ cups (240g) icing sugar

1 Preheat oven to 160°C/140°C fan-assisted. Line 18 holes of two 12-hole (40ml) deep flat-based muffin pans with paper cases.

2 Beat oil, sugar and egg in small bowl with electric mixer until thick and creamy. Stir in carrot and walnuts, then sifted flour and spice. Divide mixture into paper cases.

3 Bake cakes about 20 minutes. Stand cakes 5 minutes before turning top-side up onto wire rack to cool.

4 Meanwhile, make lemon cream cheese frosting.

5 Spoon lemon cream cheese frosting into piping bag fitted with 2cm fluted nozzle; pipe frosting onto cakes. Sprinkle cakes with combined pepitas, apricots and extra walnuts.
   LEMON CREAM CHEESE FROSTING Beat cream cheese, butter and rind in small bowl with electric mixer until light and fluffy; gradually beat in sifted icing sugar.

Orange blossom & almond cakes

preparation time 25 minutes (plus cooling time) **cooking time** 12 minutes **makes** 28

6 egg whites

185g unsalted butter, melted

2 tablespoons honey

1 tablespoon orange flower water

1 cup (120g) ground almonds

1½ cups (240g) icing sugar

½ cup (75g) plain flour

½ cup (40g) flaked almonds

HONEY SYRUP

2 tablespoons honey

1 tablespoon water

2 teaspoons orange flower water

1 Preheat oven to 180°C/160°C fan-assisted. Grease individual fluted tart moulds (30ml) with butter. Place on oven tray.

2 Place egg whites in medium bowl; whisk lightly with fork until combined. Add butter, honey, orange flower water, ground almonds, sifted icing sugar and flour; stir until combined. Half fill the tart moulds with mixture; sprinkle with almonds.

3 Bake about 12 minutes. Stand cakes 5 minutes before turning top-side up onto wire rack to cool. Repeat with remaining mixture and almonds.

4 Meanwhile, make honey syrup.

5 Serve cakes drizzled with honey syrup.
   HONEY SYRUP Combine honey and the water in small saucepan; bring to the boil. Remove from heat; stir in orange flower water. Allow to cool.

You can use any shape moulds for these little cakes. We used tart moulds bought locally, which came in sets of four. The cake mixture will be fine left to stand at room temperature if you're making the cakes in small batches. Alternatively, make 12 cakes using 12-hole (125ml) muffin pan. Divide mixture into pan holes, bake about 20 minutes.

110

Ginger powder puffs with orange cream

preparation time 25 minutes **cooking time** 10 minutes **makes** 12

2 eggs

⅓ cup (75g) caster sugar

2 tablespoons cornflour

1 tablespoon plain flour

2 tablespoons self-raising flour

1 teaspoon cocoa powder

1½ teaspoons ground ginger

¼ teaspoon ground cinnamon

ORANGE CREAM

⅔ cup (160ml) whipping cream

2 tablespoons icing sugar

1 teaspoon finely grated orange rind

1 Preheat oven to 180°C/160°C fan-assisted. Grease and flour two 12-hole (30ml) shallow round-based patty pans.

2 Beat eggs and sugar in small bowl with electric mixer until thick and creamy. Fold in triple-sifted dry ingredients. Divide mixture among pan holes. Bake about 8 minutes.

3 Working quickly, loosen edges of cakes using palette knife, then turn immediately onto baking-parchment-lined wire racks to cool.

4 Meanwhile, make orange cream by beating cream and sifted icing sugar in small bowl with electric mixer until firm peaks form; fold in rind.

5 Just before serving, sandwich puffs together with orange cream. Serve lightly dusted with sifted icing sugar.

Portuguese custard tarts

preparation time 25 minutes (plus cooling time) **cooking time** 20 minutes **makes** 24

½ cup (110g) caster sugar

2 tablespoons cornflour

3 egg yolks

¾ cup (180ml) milk

½ cup (125ml) single cream

1 vanilla pod, split lengthways

5cm strip lemon rind

1 sheet ready-rolled butter puff pastry

1 Preheat oven to 220°C/200°C fan-assisted. Grease two 12-hole (20ml) mini muffin pans.

2 Combine sugar and cornflour in medium saucepan. Gradually whisk in combined egg yolks, milk and cream.

3 Scrape vanilla seeds into custard; add rind. Stir over medium heat until mixture just comes to the boil. Remove from heat; discard rind. Cover surface of custard with cling film while making pastry cases.

4 Cut pastry sheet in half; place two halves on top of each other. Roll pastry up tightly from long side; cut log into 24 rounds.

5 Roll each pastry round on floured surface to 6cm diameter. Press pastry into pan holes.

6 Divide custard among pastry cases. Bake about 12 minutes. Turn, top-side up, onto wire rack to cool. Serve dusted with a little sifted icing sugar.

Mini toffee apples

preparation time 25 minutes (plus cooling time) cooking time 50 minutes makes 24

2 medium red apples (300g)

1 tablespoon lemon juice

3 cups (660g) caster sugar

1 cup (250ml) water

12 lollypop sticks

1 Preheat oven to 100°C/80°C fan-assisted. Grease two 12-hole (20ml) mini muffin pans.

2 Cut unpeeled apples into 0.5cm cubes; combine in small bowl with juice. Spread apple onto baking-parchment-lined oven tray. Bake, uncovered, about 40 minutes or until dried.

3 Meanwhile, stir sugar and the water in medium heavy-based saucepan over heat until sugar dissolves. Bring to the boil; boil about 10 minutes, without stirring, or until toffee turns golden brown. Remove pan from heat; allow bubbles to subside.

4 Divide apple among pan holes. Pour toffee slowly over apple; cool toffees about 10 minutes.

5 Cut each lollypop stick in half. Position half a stick, cut-side down, in centre of each toffee; cool. Using sharp, pointed knife, carefully insert down one side of each pan hole to loosen toffee from edge.

tips Gently twist the sticks then pull to remove toffees from pan. Using a saucepan with a pouring lip makes it easy to pour the hot toffee into the pans.

Orange caramels

preparation time 15 minutes (plus standing time) cooking time 10 minutes makes 24

1 cup (220g) caster sugar

90g unsalted butter

2 tablespoons golden syrup

⅓ cup (115g) glucose syrup

½ cup (125ml) sweetened condensed milk

¼ cup (60ml) single cream

2 teaspoons finely grated orange rind

¼ cup (30g) finely chopped unsalted, roasted pistachios

1 Grease two 12-hole (20ml) mini muffin pans.

2 Combine sugar, butter, syrups, condensed milk and cream in medium heavy-based saucepan; stir over heat, without boiling, until sugar dissolves. Bring to the boil; boil, stirring, about 8 minutes or until mixture is caramel in colour. Stir in rind. Remove pan from heat; allow bubbles to subside.

3 Divide mixture among pan holes; sprinkle with nuts. Stand 20 minutes before removing from pan with greased palette knife.

Passionfruit marshmallows

preparation time 20 minutes (plus cooling and standing time) cooking time 20 minutes makes 24

2 cups (160g) desiccated coconut

⅓ cup (80ml) passionfruit pulp

1 tablespoon (14g) gelatine

¼ cup (60ml) cold water

1 cup (220g) caster sugar

½ cup (125ml) hot water

1 Grease two 12-hole (20ml) mini muffin pans. Sprinkle inside of pan holes with a little of the coconut; shake pan to coat base and side of holes.

2 Strain passionfruit pulp into small bowl; discard seeds.

3 Sprinkle gelatine over the cold water in small bowl.

4 Stir passionfruit juice, sugar and the hot water in small heavy-based saucepan over heat until sugar dissolves; bring to the boil. Stir in gelatine mixture; boil, without stirring, 15 minutes. Transfer to small bowl of electric mixer; cool to lukewarm.

5 Beat mixture with electric mixer, on high speed, about 4 minutes or until mixture is thick and holds its shape.

6 Working quickly, spoon the mixture into pan holes. Sprinkle marshmallow tops with a little of the coconut to cover top evenly. Stand at room temperature about 2 hours or until firm.

7 Place remaining coconut on large tray; gently toss marshmallows to coat in coconut.

tips You need four passionfruit to get the required amount of pulp.

Turkish delight rocky road

preparation time 15 minutes cooking time 5 minutes (plus refrigeration time) makes 28

400g white eating chocolate, chopped coarsely

200g raspberry and vanilla marshmallows, chopped coarsely

200g Turkish delight, chopped finely

¾ cup (110g) toasted macadamias, chopped coarsely

1 Line two 8cm x 25cm baking tins with baking parchment, extending paper 2cm over all sides of tins.

2 Stir chocolate in medium heatproof bowl over medium saucepan of simmering water until smooth; cool 2 minutes.

3 Meanwhile, combine remaining ingredients in large bowl. Working quickly, stir in chocolate; spread mixture into tins. Refrigerate until set; cut into 1cm slices.

madeleines & morsels

Glossary

almonds, ground also known as almond meal; nuts are powdered to a coarse flour texture.

baking powder a raising agent containing starch, but mostly cream of tartar and bicarbonate of soda in the proportions of 1 teaspoon cream of tartar to ½ teaspoon bicarbonate of soda. This is equal to 2 teaspoons baking powder.

basil an aromatic herb; there are many types, but the most commonly used is sweet basil.

bicarbonate of soda also called baking soda.

bran, unprocessed the coarse outer husk of cereal grains; can be found in health food stores and supermarkets.

buttermilk fresh low-fat milk cultured to give a slightly sour, tangy taste; low-fat yogurt or milk can be substituted.

cayenne pepper thin-fleshed, long, very-hot red chilli; usually purchased dried and ground.

cheese

cheddar the most common cow's milk 'tasty' cheese; should be aged and hard.

cottage fresh, white, unripened curd cheese with a lumpy consistency and mild flavour.

cream a soft cow's-milk cheese with a fat content ranging from 14 per cent to 33 per cent.

feta a crumbly textured goat's- or sheep's-milk cheese with a sharp, salty taste.

mozzarella a semi-soft cheese with a delicate, fresh taste; has a low melting point and stringy texture when hot.

parmesan a sharp-tasting, dry, hard Italian cheese, made from skimmed or semi-skimmed milk and aged for at least a year.

chickpeas also called garbanzos, hummus or channa; an irregularly round, sandy-coloured legume.

chives related to the onion and leek, with subtle onion flavour.

chocolate

chips hold their shape in baking.

dark eating made of cocoa liquor, cocoa butter and sugar.

hazelnut spread we use Nutella.

milk eating most popular eating chocolate, mild and very sweet; similar in make-up to dark, but with the addition of milk solids.

white eating contains no cocoa solids, deriving its sweet flavour from cocoa butter. Is very sensitive to heat.

chorizo a sausage of Spanish origin; made of coarsely ground pork and seasoned with garlic and chillies.

cinnamon dried inner bark of the shoots of the cinnamon tree. Available as a stick or ground.

cloves can be used whole or in ground form. Has a strong scent and taste so should be used minimally.

cocoa powder cocoa beans that have been fermented, roasted, shelled, ground into powder then cleared of most of the fat content.

coconut

desiccated unsweetened and concentrated, dried finely shredded.

flaked dried flaked coconut flesh.

milk unsweetened coconut milk available in cans.

shredded thin strips of dried coconut.

coffee-flavoured liqueur we use either Kahlua or Tia Maria coffee-flavoured liqueur.

condensed milk a canned milk product consisting of milk with more than half the water content removed and sugar added to the milk that remains.

coriander dried a fragrant herb; coriander seeds and ground coriander must never be used to replace fresh coriander or vice versa. The tastes are completely different.

cornflour also known as cornstarch; used as a thickening agent in cooking.

cornmeal flour ground from dried corn. Ground to fine, medium, and coarse consistencies, it is the main ingredient of cornbread.

cream we used fresh cream in this book, unless otherwise stated. Also known as pure cream and pouring cream; has no additives unlike commercially thickened cream. Minimum fat content 35%.

soured a thick commercially-cultured soured cream. Minimum fat content 35%.

whipping a cream that contains a thickener. Has a minimum fat content of 35 per cent.

cumin available both ground and as whole seeds; cumin has a warm, earthy, rather strong flavour.

curry powder a blend of ground spices; choose mild or hot to suit your taste and the recipe.

date fruit of the date palm tree, eaten fresh or dried, on their own or in prepared dishes. About 4cm to 6cm in length, oval and plump, thin-skinned, with a honey-sweet flavour and sticky texture.

dulce de leche a caramel sauce made from milk and sugar. Can be used straight from the jar for cheesecakes, slices and tarts. Has similar qualities to sweetened condensed milk, only a thicker, caramel consistency; great to use in caramel desserts.

essences are synthetically produced substances used in small amounts to impart their respective flavours to foods. An extract is made by actually extracting the flavour from a food product. In the case of vanilla, pods are soaked, usually in alcohol, to capture the authentic flavour. Both extracts and essences will keep indefinitely if stored in a cool dark place.

figs small, soft, pear-shaped fruit with a sweet pulpy flesh full of tiny edible seeds. Vary in skin and flesh colour according to type, not ripeness; when ripe, figs should be unblemished and bursting with flavour; nectar beads at the base indicate when a fig is at its best. Figs may also be glacéd, dried or canned in sugar syrup.

flour

plain all-purpose flour.

self-raising plain flour sifted with baking powder (a raising agent consisting mainly of 2 parts cream of tartar to 1 part bicarbonate of soda) in the proportion of 150g flour to 2 level teaspoons baking powder.

wholemeal also known as wholewheat flour; milled with the wheat germ so is higher in fibre and more nutritional than plain flour.

gelatine we used powdered gelatine; also available in sheet form known as leaf gelatine.

ginger, stem fresh ginger root preserved in sugar syrup.

glacé fruit fruit such as cherries, peaches, pineapple, orange and citron cooked in heavy sugar syrup then dried.

glucose syrup also known as liquid glucose.

golden syrup a by-product of refined sugarcane; pure maple syrup or honey can be substituted.

hazelnuts, ground made by grinding hazelnuts to a coarse flour texture for use in baking or as a thickening agent.

macadamias native to Australia, a rich and buttery nut; store in refrigerator because of its high oil content.

maple syrup distilled from the sap of maple trees found only in Canada and parts of North America. Maple-flavoured syrup is not an adequate substitute for the real thing.

mixed spice a blend of ground spices usually consisting of cinnamon, allspice and nutmeg.

mustard, dijon a pale brown, distinctively flavoured fairly mild French mustard.

nutmeg dried nut of an evergreen tree; available in ground form or you can grate your own with a fine grater.

oil

olive mono-unsaturated; made from the pressing of tree-ripened olives. Extra virgin and virgin are the best, obtained from the first pressings of the olive, while extra light or light refers to the taste, not fat levels.

vegetable Any number of oils sourced from plants rather than animal fats.

orange-flavoured liqueur you can use any orange-flavoured liqueur: Grand Marnier, Cointreau, Curaçao are all suitable.

orange flower water concentrated flavouring made from orange blossoms.

oregano also known as wild marjoram; has a woody stalk with clumps of tiny, dark green leaves that have a pungent, peppery flavour and are used fresh or dried.

pancetta an Italian salt-cured pork roll, usually cut from the belly; used, chopped, in cooked dishes to add flavours. Bacon can be substituted.

paprika ground dried red pepper; available sweet, smoked or hot.

passionfruit a small tropical fruit, native to Brazil, comprised of a tough dark-purple skin surrounding edible black sweet-sour seeds.

pecans native to the United States; golden-brown, buttery and rich. Good in savoury and sweet dishes; especially good in salads.

pesto a paste made from fresh basil, oil, garlic, pine nuts and parmesan.

pistachios pale green, delicately flavoured nut inside hard off-white shells. To peel, soak shelled nuts in boiling water about 5 minutes; drain, then pat dry.

polenta a flour-like cereal made of ground corn (maize); similar to cornmeal but finer and lighter in colour.

poppy seeds small, dried, bluish-grey seeds of the poppy plant. Poppy seeds have a crunchy texture and a nutty flavour. Available whole or ground.

prosciutto salted-cured, air-dried (unsmoked), pressed ham; usually sold in paper-thin slices, ready to eat.

rolled oats traditional whole oat grains that have been steamed and flattened. Not to be confused with the quick-cook variety.

sambal oelek a salty paste made from ground chillies.

sesame seeds black and white are the most common of these tiny oval seeds; a good source of calcium.

sugar

brown an extremely soft, fine granulated sugar retaining molasses for its deep colour and flavour.

caster also known as superfine or finely granulated table sugar.

demerara small-grained golden-coloured crystal sugar.

icing also known as confectioners' sugar or powdered sugar.

raw natural brown granulated sugar.

sweet chilli sauce mild, Thai sauce made from red chillies, sugar, garlic and vinegar.

vanilla

essence obtained from vanilla beans infused in alcohol and water.

extract obtained from vanilla beans infused in water; a non-alcoholic version of essence.

pod dried long, thin pod from a tropical golden orchid grown in central and South America and Tahiti; the minuscule black seeds inside the bean are used to impart a distinctively sweet vanilla flavour.

Index

index

Conversion charts

measures

The cup and spoon measurements used in this book are metric: one measuring cup holds approximately 250ml; one metric tablespoon holds 20ml; one metric teaspoon holds 5ml.

All cup and spoon measurements are level. The most accurate way of measuring dry ingredients is to weigh them. When measuring liquids, use a clear glass or plastic jug with the metric markings.

We use large eggs with an average weight of 60g. This book contains recipes for dishes made with raw or lightly cooked eggs. These should be avoided by vulnerable people such as pregnant and nursing mothers, invalids, the elderly, babies and young children.

dry measures

METRIC	IMPERIAL
15g	½oz
30g	1oz
60g	2oz
90g	3oz
125g	4oz (¼lb)
155g	5oz
185g	6oz
220g	7oz
250g	8oz (½lb)
280g	9oz
315g	10oz
345g	11oz
375g	12oz (¾lb)
410g	13oz
440g	14oz
470g	15oz
500g	16oz (1lb)
750g	24oz (1½lb)
1kg	32oz (2lb)

liquid measures

METRIC	IMPERIAL
30ml	1 fluid oz
60ml	2 fluid oz
100ml	3 fluid oz
125ml	4 fluid oz
150ml	5 fluid oz (¼ pint/1 gill)
190ml	6 fluid oz
250ml	8 fluid oz
300ml	10 fluid oz (½ pint)
500ml	16 fluid oz
600ml	20 fluid oz (1 pint)
1000ml (1 litre)	1¾ pints

length measures

METRIC	IMPERIAL
3mm	⅛ in
6mm	¼in
1cm	½in
2cm	¾in
2.5cm	1in
5cm	2in
6cm	2½in
8cm	3in
10cm	4in
13cm	5in
15cm	6in
18cm	7in
20cm	8in
23cm	9in
25cm	10in
28cm	11in
30cm	12in (1ft)

oven temperatures

These oven temperatures are only a guide for conventional ovens. For fan-assisted ovens, check the manufacturer's manual.

	°C (CELSIUS)	°F (FAHRENHEIT)	GAS MARK
Very low	120	250	½
Low	150	275-300	1-2
Moderately low	160	325	3
Moderate	180	350-375	4-5
Moderately hot	200	400	6
Hot	220	425-450	7-8
Very hot	240	475	9

This book is published in 2010 by Octopus Publishing Group Limited based on materials licensed it by ACP Magazines Ltd, a division of PBL Media Pty Limited

54 Park St, Sydney
GPO Box 4088, Sydney, NSW 2001
phone (02) 9282 8618;
fax (02) 9267 9438
acpbooks@acpmagazines.com.au;
www.acpbooks.com.au

OCTOPUS BOOKS

Design: Chris Bell
Food Director: Pamela Clark

Published and Distributed in the United Kingdom by Octopus Publishing Group Limited

Endeavour House
189 Shaftesbury Avenue
London WC2H 8JY
United Kingdom
phone + 44 (0) 207 632 5400;
fax + 44 (0) 207 632 5405

aww@octopusbooks.co.uk; www.octopusbooks.co.uk
www.australian-womens-weekly.com

Printed and bound in China

International foreign language rights,
Brian Cearnes, ACP Books
bcearnes@acpmagazines.com.au

A catalogue record for this book is available from the British Library.

ISBN 978-1-907428-05-0
© ACP Magazines Ltd 2010
ABN 18 053 273 546

This publication is copyright. No part of it may be reproduced or transmitted in any form without the written permission of the Publisher.

To order books:
telephone LBS on 01903 828 503
order online at www.australian-womens-weekly.com
or www.octopusbooks.co.uk